Steeples in Metropolis

Steeples in Metropolis

ROBERT G. HOWES

PFLAUM PRESS • DAYTON, OHIO • 1969

Library of Congress Catalog Card Number: 69-20171
Copyright © 1969 by Robert G. Howes
Printed in the United States of America

Preface

At the outset, two points need to be made clear. First, this is not a complete study of the Church in metropolis. I have never met a total expert in either religion or metropolis, and I do not propose myself as one. Nor is this book intended as a compendium of comment on all that churchmen are doing everywhere across America in metropolis. I am well aware of significant activity in Washington, D.C., Chicago, and Camden on an urban scale. I am well aware of significant activity in New York and Los Angeles on a regional scale. There are many other programs and projects underway at various stages and in various locations with which I am more or less acquainted. I recognize them, but I do not propose to describe or evaluate them. This book is intended to explore the general, more comprehensive role of religion in metropolis from the point of view of a planning priest. If the Baltimore experience receives special notice, it is only because I was personally a part of it. If the local, neighborhood, parochial presence of the Church in metropolis is given rather less than more attention, it is only because my own emphasis is overall rather than local. Hopefully, other churchmen in metropolis and other planners concerned with the impact of religion on metropolis will be helped by this expression of a point of view which is at once religious and secular.

Second, I must thank many for the birth of this book, though the conclusions here must be my sole responsibility. I am grateful to David Loeks, immediate past president of the American Institute of Planners, who introduces the book and whose keen sense of the planner's quandary and promise in metropolis has long inspired me; to Lawrence Cardinal Shehan and Right Reverend Monsignor Joseph M. Nelligan, who commissioned the Baltimore Urban Parish Study, and to my staff colleagues in that study for their insights and their constructive sweat with me; and to Mrs. Dorothy Lowe for her secretarial patience and performance with a changing manuscript. Special gratitude is due my friends, Rev. John J. McKenzie, O.S.A., M.C.P., of Villanova University, who is responsible for the cover photograph and who encouraged me throughout, and Rev. Leo R. Sands, C.S.B., of the Theology Department at St. John Fisher College, Rochester, New York, for his willingness to listen as these pages grew and for the spiritual sstrength he shared with me again and again as the growing occurred.

Semantically, there are two points which perhaps need to be made. I have used the word *Church* to refer to Roman Catholicism, *churches* to refer to religious institutions generally —Jewish, Protestant, and Roman Catholic. I am aware of, and an early chapter will explain, the difference between metropolis and megalopolis. I have, however, elected to use the former rather than the latter throughout, though at times megalopolis may be more accurate. I mean by *metropolis* the so-called "central city" and its suburbs, the urban area, the metropolitan region.

For the rest, if these pages say anything to a religion which is increasingly concerned with planning, and facilitate what I am convinced is one of the most important dialogues in metropolis today, that between churchmen and planners, I shall have succeeded.

Acknowledgments

The author wishes to thank the following publishers, publications and organizations for permission to reprint copyrighted material.

From *In the Clearing* by Robert Frost. Copyright © 1956, 1962 by Robert Frost. Reprinted by permission of Holt, Rinehart and Winston, Inc.

From *The Living City* by Frank Lloyd Wright. Copyright © 1958. Reprinted by permission of the publisher, Horizon Press.

Commonweal for quotation from the editorial in the February 2, 1968, issue.

Daedalus for Daniel Callahan's "The Quest for Social Relevance" in the Winter, 1967, issue.

Urban America for Donald Canty's "City" in September, 1967, issue.

Town and Country Planning Association, London, England, for quotation from October, 1960, issue of *Town and Country Planning Review*.

Reprinted by permission of the *Journal of the American Institute of Planners*:

"The Housing of Relocated Families" by Chester Hartman, Vol. 30, No. 4 (November, 1964)

"Interpretations: The Planner as a Bureaucrat" by Norman

Beckman, Vol. 30, No. 4 (November, 1964)

"A View of Ethics and Planning" by Robert C. Hoover, Vol. 27, No. 4 (November, 1961)

"Advocacy and Pluralism in Planning" by Paul Davidoff, Vol. 31, No. 4 (November, 1965).

American Society of Planning Officials for quotations from ASPO material.

American Institute of Planners for quotations from the 1965 AIP Conference Proceedings.

Table of Contents

Introduction

"The Church's response to the urban crisis? It's just not living up to its potential role! Where's its relevance?" He said it with a resigned shrug, mixed with just a tinge of uneasiness. Clearly, my young activist friend preferred to move the conversation to things he felt he could do something about, like changing the world.

That this attitude exists and indeed pervades much of contemporary society, comes as a surprise to no one, especially the churchman committed to resuscitating his institution's mission of renewal and redemption. What *is* surprising is that so many would-be world changers, including the planners, appear willing, with varying degrees of regret, to accept the Church's present condition as a given, rather than as a variable that can and must be changed.

Why surprising? Consider for a moment the mission of the planner. What's he up to? Stripped of its rhetoric, his job is to help improve man's welfare by helping to improve his environment in its several dimensions. The planner's success is absolutely dependent on the willingness of people to define and pursue the common good. Such pursuit raises ethical and moral questions of a fundamental nature. Questions such as, Who gets what? Who does what to whom? and, Who says so? tug and rend the seams of our polarizing society. Too frequently, the answer comes back as either "I've got mine, Jack!" or, in cases where he didn't, "Burn, baby, burn!"

How, then, can the quest for commonwealth possibly succeed if, in fact, we live in a world which celebrates me-first-manship and relegates the "I'm third" ethic to the scoutmaster and the Sunday school teacher? These are hard questions and they demand hard answers of the world changers. A basic assumption of optimism concerning the radical perfectability of man is in order. If the assumption cannot be made, why bother? Are not we just playing a deadly little game of nursemaid and doctor, applying bandaids to society's terminal cancer?

"Wait a minute," the churchman might reply, "I've already crossed that bridge! Man's perfectability is no hang-up with me. That happens to be the name of my particular game!" The point, exactly! The difference between churchmen and other world changers is that the clergy makes no bones about this basic assumption, it is an article of faith, whereas most of the rest of us are either unaware of its existence, or unwilling to concede the true extent of its operational relevance.

And so we come to a basic point in Father Howes' gospel: planners and churchmen and all the other world changers concerned with improving man's welfare, really do need each other. We have been working different sides of the same street and it is time to cross over and turn up the tempo and the temperature of the multilog. Everyone needs all the help he can get.

At the core of his message is the key question of how to get meaningful involvement of religion in the life of the metropolis. The moral issues and explication of values which emerge from the planner's examination of the implications of alternatives certainly bears on this question. We are also reminded that the urban crisis is but an expression of a larger crisis of spirit, and that it is the special business of the clergy to help individuals and society to grapple with it.

If we begin to act on the postulate that self-renewal leads to societial renewal, what then shall be the basis for our renewed sense of community, so urgently needed? The planner might respond: "It's our essential interaction and interdependence in the use of our limited environmental resources." (How's that for planner talk?) The churchman could proclaim: "It's our shared relationship with God!" Robert Howes, the planner-priest urges that it is both, and in ethical terms, that they are of the same piece of cloth.

No crier of doom or despair, his analysis and prescription suggests that today's woes can be viewed as the birth pangs of a new era, rather than the death throes of the old. For a planner, this is good news, for our interests tend toward the obstetric rather than the geriatric. Moreover, it does not hurt to remind us that there is plenty of midwifing to go around for everyone.

Apparently planners and churchmen are going to have to get to know each other better if the steeples in the metropolis are to make their point. Thank God for this tentmaker who tells it like it is to both the secular and the religious alike.

C. David Loeks, A.I.P.
President of the American Institute
of Planners, 1964-1966.

Steeples in Metropolis

Christian Perspective

ONE

... the modern world shows itself ... capable of the noblest deeds or the foulest; before it lies the path to freedom or to slavery, to progress or retreat, to brotherhood or hatred. ... the forces which he [man] has unleashed ... can enslave him or minister to him.—*Constitution on the Church in the Modern World,* paragraph 9.

The religious motivation in metropolis is fundamentally incarnational. The goal is the spirit opening in and through the concrete and the congestion, the plans and the people. Under a kind of divine mandate, religion must be actively concerned with writing the corporal and spiritual works of mercy into the soul and shape of cities. Robert Frost expressed it best when he wrote:

But God's own descent
Into flesh was meant
As a demonstration
That the supreme merit
Lay in risking spirit
In substantiation.

3

Spirit enters flesh
And for all it's worth
Charges into earth
In birth after birth
Ever fresh and fresh.
We may take the view
That its derring-do
Thought of in the large
Is one mighty charge
On our human part
Of the soul's ethereal
Into the material.[1]

Whether the city is secular or not is not the real question. The real question is the meaningful involvement of religion in metropolis. Whether its reasoning for such involvement is accepted or not by the community, the real question is whether religion can become a positive, daring presence, helping to lead the forces of confidence in the radical improvement of urban man.

The task of reducing this high purpose to manageable dimensions requires much thought and commitment. As with any other corporate body injecting itself into society, religious bodies must first explore the terrain in which they propose to intervene and consider those who already occupy such terrain. They must discover simple obtainable goals within the complex mass of metropolis. Finally, they must ponder these goals to determine the distinction between the ideal and the real. But they must ponder them passionately aware of flaming streets and broken barriers.

---

[1]Robert Frost, *In the Clearing* (New York: Holt, Rinehart and Winston, 1962), p. 7.

My context at this point is Christianity in the United States today as a civic fact, and megalopolis as it exists and predictably will exist over the next few decades. My concern is with the mode, the immediate motivation, and the mechanics of religion in the city rather than with the wider theology of interaction.

The term *megalopolis* was introduced into the contemporary planning vocabulary by Patrick Geddes in Britain in 1913. Growing cities, he believed, tend to pass through five stages. At the start, there is the polis, the small community. This becomes metropolis, larger but still healthy. Megalopolis follows: Geddes calls it unhealthy, oversized, and with a tendency toward megalomania. Megalopolis is succeeded by parasitopolis, which will drain an entire country of its lifeblood. The process terminates in pathopolis, a diseased, more and more abandoned relic. Clearly, with well over half the American people crowding into two percent of our land area, we have arrived at megalopolis. Clearly, the processes or urban giantism continue. Clearly the threat of pathopolis confronts us.

Meeting on the Greek isle of Delos on July 12, 1963, thirty-four urban experts from across the globe issued an urban declaration. They pointed up some of the chief challenges of megalopolis:

1. As he moves more and more into urban areas, man faces "the deepest and widest revolution ever to overtake" him. This revolution has two aspects. "Science and technology determine more and more of the processes of human living." The technical options of an environment subject as never before to human control "present themselves in every field as a danger matched by an even greater opportunity." At the same time "man's" social behavior is profoundly modified."

2. The problems of clotting urbanism grow in geometric progression. "World population increases by two per cent a year, urban population by over four per cent. In the next forty years, more urban construction will take place than hitherto in the whole history of man."

3. To meet this problem effectively, "we feel the need for the most far-reaching reform and reinforcement of existing institutions and procedures."

4. To meet this problem effectively, we shall have to build new coherences, new systems of thought and action into our schools, our profession, and our government. "The application of the basic sciences to human welfare has been fragmented. They have dealt with parts of man . . . not with the whole man, not with man in community."

But all this is the lofty view. Down close to it megalopolis is a teeming intricacy. Teilhard de Chardin speaks of a "malady of multitude and immensity."[2] Lewis Mumford details repeatedly the negativeness in urban giantism.

The metropolis in its final stage of development, becomes a collective contrivance for making this irrational system work, and for giving those who are in reality its victims the illusion of power, wealth and felicity, of standing at the very pinnacle of human achievement. But in actual fact their lives are constantly in peril, their wealth is tasteless and ephemeral, their leisure is sensationally monotonous, and their pathetic felicity is tainted by constraint, well-justified anticipation of violence and sudden death.[3]

---

[2]Teilhard de Chardin, *The Phenomenon of Man* (New York: Harper and Row Torchbook, 1965), p. 228.
[3]Lewis Mumford, *City in History* (New York: Harcourt, Brace, 1961), p. 546.

Barbara Ward suggests that for all its blessings, spread city may be indeed a lethal weapon. Frank Lloyd Wright laments "the nonunderstanding in overgrown urban life."[4] He adds:

Such frantic energy pours through this haphazard money-mountain made by the mile to pile up and confuse man and materials; here and there ruthless; drenched by what relentless ambition has wrung from our abounding national resources.[5]

He continues:

. . . and the citizen is now so far gone that he easily mistakes pig-piling and crowding of big business for eminence or excellence; mistakes the push-button powers of the machine age for his own powers and finds hectic excitement in urban uproar and the vertigo of verticality. The more citified he becomes the less civilized he is; the more this racing of the iron horse into the inferiority of conformity grows characteristic of his weakness. Roaring tumults of congestion emphasize terrific collisions of power; explosions of grinding mechanical forces in this whirling vortex, urban exaggeration; in these the rich whirling dervish, thinks he sees his own greatness.[6]

Another architect is equally disturbed.

The modern city is obscene. . . . People currently are fleeing from this man-created carcinoma in the center of the scene to the questionable safety of the suburbs, returning warily at night for social nourishment when the purple shadows of the evening hide its bleeding ugliness.[7]

---

[4]Frank Lloyd Wright, *The Living City* (New York: Mentor, 1963), p. 58.
[5]*Ibid.*, p. 54.
[6]*Ibid.*, p. 58.
[7]Thomas K. Fitzpatrick, "The Church in the City of Tomorrow" in *AIA Journal* (November, 1959), p. 17.

Vertically in its structures and its governance, horizontally over multiplying random acres, fiscally, in its moving majorities and its penned up minorities, topically as programs and moneys to solve it, and as angry poor mass in its streets, the problem of metropolis becomes daily more intricate. None of this is meant to counsel despair. All of it is meant to point up the frightful seriousness of the task of spiritual intervention in metropolis. In fact, for every Cassandra about cities, there is at least half an optimist and part of a Pollyanna!

Episcopal Bishop Moore is certainly correct when he warns that religion "must not become discouraged by the confusion which often seems so overwhelming,"[8] even though former Vice-President Hubert Humphrey, in speaking of "the galloping muddle of our cities," notes that "the world is becoming more complex; its problems more impossible for ordinary people to resolve."

There are at least two corollaries to this dilemma. Harvey Cox puts his finger on one of them when he notices a conflict between the aspirations and the situation of the common man in metropolitan politics. More and more, he remarks, civic decision requires expertise of an increasingly high and interdisciplinary nature. He speaks of "the remystification of politics. Once again politics has become distant, mysterious and foreboding."[9] Yet, at the same time he sees the rise of a new breed of "participatory democrats": "A whole society and all of its institutions are now subject to thoughtful change and shaping, and every person, even

---

[8]E. Paul Moore, *The Church Reclaims the City* (Greenwich, Connecticut: Seabury Press, 1964), p. 110.
[9]Harvey Cox, in *Technology and Culture in Perspective* (Cambridge, Massachusetts: The Church Society for College Work, 1966), p. 7.

the tinkers and the cobblers, somehow has a role in the shaping of that society."[10] There is, says the Associate Director of Georgia Tech's School of Industrial Management, Dr. R. Earl Green, a growing and angry conflict between the "opportunity and expectations of urban man."[11] Bernard J. Coughlin, S.J., Dean of St. Louis University's School of Social Work, suggests that in such a society as this quick panaceas are worse than invalid:

> History is replete with charlatans who made an easy living off the simple-minded who want a single, rule-of-the-thumb solution to the world's problems. Social philosophies that attempt to organize society according to a single, one-sided absolute concept are doomed to failure.[12]

Pious oversimplification simply will not help. It may, indeed, hinder if and as it results in uncompromising polarizations.

In short, the fact of complication, the sheer difficulty of finding a really effective participatory method in metropolis, and the urgency of action cannot be ignored. More than ever the structural missionary is needed, the churchman who, gifted with competence as well as charisma, can combine understanding with the white warm light of a simple love.

When he was challenged to an "ethical inquiry and discourse" about urban renewal in West Philadelphia recently, Leo Molinaro, then President of the West Philadelphia Association replied with a challenge of his own to the challenging churchman:

---

[10]*Ibid.*, p. 4.
[11]Address to the American Institute of Urban and Regional Affairs, Atlanta, Georgia, May 8, 1968.
[12]Address to the Conference on Religion in the City, St. Mary's Jesuit Theologate, St. Mary's Kansas, November 26, 1965.

We must submit to the discipline of fact-finding before attempting an evaluation of the situation . . . [his] statement does not do so. . . . At best this is a caricature of the facts . . . [he] employs heavily charged adjectives, exaggerations and omissions, all calculated to produce a strong emotional reaction. This is hardly conducive to creating a mood for ethical discourse.[13]

I do not vouch for the accuracy of Mr. Molinaro's estimate. I do suggest that this kind of estimate underwrites the absolute urgency for careful analysis as well as impassioned proclamation when the Church intervenes in specific situations in metropolis. The apostolate of correct facts, of meetings and positive sweat may well be as important in our time as the apostolate of protest. It was perhaps of this type of apostolate that Pius XII spoke: "To know how to go slowly, how to await the proper moment and measure what is said and what is asked—this is the first and indispensable qualification for apostolic action."[14]

Robert Frost's suggestion that the problem of our time is "how to crowd, but still be kind"[15] is clearly apropos. If kindness is a concern of the spirit of man and the churchman is eminently called to pronounce on it, crowdedness and the remedies for it involve situations in which secular study and solution are necessary. The churchman is no more qualified by the fact of his office to speak to the latter than is the planner qualified by the fact of his office to adjudicate the former. The technological response to crowdedness and the spiritual imperatives of kindness must be combined in

---

[13]*Colloquy*, the Christian Association at the University of Pennsylvania (April, 1967), p. 22.
[14]To the Pastors of Rome, March 10, 1955.
[15]Frost, p. 21.

one continuous effort. Their different motivations and their separate skills must be blended in one united action. The total problem can only be resolved in a common endeavor. A systems approach is imperatively required.[16]

At the other end of our subject relationship, Christianity itself faces a great convergence and divergence of questions as to what it is and how it is. We have by no means reached a plateau of response to these interior questions. Perhaps we never shall. Inevitably the character and reach of our interim responses will affect our mission in megalopolis. One thing is clear. Religion is a plural presence in time. Religion is structure, institution, gospel, pastors and people, education, inspiration and liturgy. Out of all of these, a coherent approach must be built.

The problem of internal structuring for civics is multilateral. A systems approach to that problem must reckon with situations which are not simple, not new, in many cases, but newly big, not subject to edge-of-time solutions. This approach must also reckon with a serious and radical flux in at least four areas: 1) an uncertainty as to the role of the pastor, the committed Christian, and the institution in urban community; 2) an uncertainty as to the ideal and even the

---

[16]There are many definitions of "the systems approach." At the Portland, Oregon, convention of the American Institute of Planners, in August, 1966, Mr. W. L. Rogers of the Aerojet-General Corporation defined it in these terms:

As used in the aerospace industry, this old but new technology follows the general pattern of: (1) establishment of mission requirements; (2) derivation of general system requirements; (3) separation of the system into identifiable components and subsystems; (4) system analysis to identify optimum combinations of subsystems; (5) establishment of design and operational criteria; (6) testing to determine that system objectives have been met; and finally (7), manufacturing, assembling, and operating the system.

See, for further discussion: *Environment for Man* (Bloomington, Indiana: Indiana University Press, 1967), pp. 3-11, 260-269.

possible shape and psyche of spread city; 3) an uncertainty as to how urban programs and technology will in the long- and short-run reform the life of man in megalopolis; 4) an uncertainty as to the impact of massed anger outside normal politics on the course of national processes and the national conscience.

"The past is prologue," so reads the phrase on the Archives Building in Washington. To project, one must first look back. Mumford writes: "Without a long running start in history we shall not have the momentum needed, in our own consciousness, to take a sufficiently bold leap into the future."[17] The literature probing Christianity's impact on society is substantial. Generally, lines of comment run fairly constant. At least since the Industrial Revolution, civic policy in nominally Christian communities has often failed to put into practice the mandates of justice and charity which lie at the heart of the Christian gospel. Individual Christians have simply not, in sufficient numbers or with sufficient perseverence, translated the ideas they should have found in their gospels and at their altars into civic reality. Christian religious institutions have too frequently stood aside from societal change and immediate misery. Religion, as Emile Durkheim noted in 1922 (and as the Lynds plus many others repeat), embraces "continually . . . a smaller part of social life."[18] Writing in 1959, Catholic sociologist Dennis Clark states bluntly:

Catholic social ideas remain theoretical and frequently the attitude of the . . . body social and the formal Catholic institu-

---

[17]Mumford, p. 3.
[18]Emil Durkheim, *De La Division du Travail Social* (Paris, 1922), p. 143.

tional outlook in its relation to city affairs is one of blandly independent self-concern and self-development with occasional fits of agitated obstructionism.[19]

Fully to catalogue our mistakes would require a lengthy and painful excursion. But simply to note them should suffice. What is most required of religion in metropolis is, in any case, not the monotonous drone of *ex post facto mea culpas*, but rather trumpet calls to positive achievement. Over the years we Christians have often been spasmodic off-and-on citizens. We have often dodged the real issues, becoming, as Peter Marshall once put it, like divers in suits capable of great depth, moving around pulling the plugs out of bath tubs! We have often been preach-and-run Christians, raising issues with instant righteousness and then running away from them. We have often been theoretical, tall-in-our-dream-tower Christians, Alices in an irrelevant wonderland, proposing ideal remedies for an ideal mankind. We have often stood denominational in the presence of problems which are utterly non-denominational. We have often approached community only in the dimension of our own self-interest, like a fortress threatened physically as well as morally by a surrounding bitter countryside. As the Reverend E. Paul Musselman puts it, we have engaged in "corral Christianity—riding around shouting words of encouragement at each other and singing ancient hymns saying, 'there's hostiles out in them thar hills.'"[20] And through it all there survives a strange feeling that somehow reason and faith

---

[19]Dennis Clark, *Cities in Crisis* (New York: Sheed and Ward, 1959), pp. 90, 91.

[20]Address at Civic Forum, sponsored by The Clergy Committee on the Community, All Saints Church, Worcester, Massachusetts, February 8, 1962.

are incongruous, as if, by better tooling up our structures and informing our leaders in secular wisdoms, we destroy their inspiration and impede their graces.

More recently, there are evidences of new maturity. The National Conference on Race and Religion is one instance. There are others, nationally and locally. We begin to appreciate the need for technicians in community. The first glow of our spoken commitment wears off and we start to face the fact that wishing simply will not make things so, that we must move from commitment to the painful, slower processes of involvement in real-life sweat and struggle.

As government programming reaches out to new horizons of justice and compassion toward the urban disadvantaged, at the same time our own interest in and, at least initial, capacity for cooperation increase. In Roman Catholicism for the first time, in the Center for Applied Research in the Apostolate, we boast a national religious agency dedicated to scientific self-analysis. It is not yet by any means certain how the Center will develop. Its existence is important. However, there remain at least these conceptual difficulties:

I. In Teilhard de Chardin's view, there is a without and a within of things, and a mutuality between them. Architects like to say that form follows function. We have simply not in the Church suited our old without to our new within. We have simply not yet shaped our forms to meet our new functions of relevance. It will take time, and we are beginning, but we have many miles and many reformations ahead before the religious organism is really adjusted to its new ecology.

II. We are seriously deficient in research, analysis, and ongoing communication. Not enough of us, with enough consistency and competence, submit the tentatives toward relevance with which we are disparately surrounded, to dispassionate assessment, cutting here and filling there as the need may be. Nor have we as yet established that adequacy of communication between urban Church experimenters which could translate a valid experience anywhere into a useful guide everywhere.

III. The debate is by no means over between the personalists and the institutionalists.[21] Is it the role of religion merely to inspire its congregants to vote wisely and involve themselves as free agents in community? If it is, does not the danger arise that we repeat a tactic which through centuries has quite obviously not succeeded in reforming the world? In the "Colloquy" series referred to above, Mr. L. William Yolton, Acting Director of the Christian Association at the University of Pennsylvania, writes, "[We] are constantly disappointed that it [i.e., the Church] deals primarily with individuals and does not comprehend the problems of corporate responsibility."[22] Robert McAfee Brown aptly adds:

The evangelization of individuals is never enough. It takes a lifetime to convert even a small group of individuals after

---

[21]In a sermon entitled "Vertical or Horizontal Religion," delivered at the National Presbyterian Church, Washington, D.C., on April 28, 1968, the pastor, Rev. Dr. Edward L. R. Elston, said in part:
It is the essence of the Gospel that changed people can make a better world. Changed people with the dynamic message of the Gospel went out across an ancient world once upon a time, not with a sociological blueprint, but by proclaiming the good news of the Gospel of God . . . [they] did in fact transform a . . . world. . . . It is one thing for an individual Christian in the light of his own insights and wisdom to become involved in the affairs of the world and make his Christian witness there. It is quite another thing when some men attempt to make their own views of economics, politics, and society the views of the whole Church and commit the Church as an institution to such views.
Full text in *Congressional Record*, May 9, 1968, p. E 4029.
[22]*Colloquy*, p. 17.

which the process must begin all over again, while the injustices of society are studiously being ignored . . . To convert a man living in substandard housing, without concern for the appalling conditions under which he must raise his family, is to betray a deficient vision of the concerns of the gospel for that man's life.[23]

Should the institutional Church and its corporate spokesmen, whether lay or clerical, specifically back legislation and public programs? "Because the Church is an influential organizational unit in community life, it cannot shift its responsibilities to its individual lay and clerical members . . . It must as a corporate body address itself unselfishly to community needs."[24] If corporate action is indicated, we cannot escape further questions. Who rightfully speaks for a religious institution? Must the matter be adjudicated by majority vote; and if not, by what singular gift of superior judgment does one pastor or body or lay group presume to know better than the mass of congregants what is right and what wrong in a complex political context? While this debate between personalism and institutionalism continues, its resolution is at least in theory simple. What seems to be indicated is not a polarization, an either-or dichotomy, but a continuum running from religion as an informed institution intervening positively in major matters of collective morality to religion as publicly inspired and responsibly activating its single congregants.

I suggest that our principal civic objectives as Christians

---

[23]Robert McAfee Brown, *Spirit of Protestantism* (New York: Oxford University Press, 1961), p. 20.

[24]Haskell M. Miller, *Compassion and Community* (New York: Association Press), p. 193.

in metropolis are two. We must, first, help restore hope to metropolitan man. We must, second, propose or at least be effectively involved in the proposition of a viable vision to metropolitan society. Corbusier put the initial need well: "Our constant aim which we must pursue with patience and cunning must be to throw out of action all the forces that make for the opposite of Joy—that is to say—Despair, Despairing Cities! The Despair of Cities!"[25]

If he honestly believes what modern Christianity prays and preaches, the Christian should be one of the most model citizens in every model neighborhood. We must become a great radiance of practical optimism about cities. We must inform man of his centrality in creation and of his option, however difficult it in fact may be to exercise it, to control his urban destiny. But we cannot stop here. The encyclical *Mater et Magistra* warned us that religion must do more than preach patience to the poor and charity to the rich. So, too, there must be more to the Christian perspective in metropolis than pious good humor. It is quite true, as Baptist pastor Younger suggests, that religion should be a questioning presence in a renewing city. We must raise the fundamental human questions. He writes:

The most important role for the church to play in the process of urban renewal is not the adaptation of its own life and program to deal with the results of urban renewal policies. Rather it is to raise questions about the policies themselves while they are still in the making. The crucial task for the church is to raise the question of values.[26]

---

[25]Corbusier, *The City of Tomorrow and Its Planning* (New York: Reynal and Hitchcock, 1945), p. 55.
[26]George D. Younger, *The Church and Urban Renewal* (Philadelphia: Lippincott, 1965), p. 15.

It is also quite true, as it has been for centuries, that men of religion must note and stand eloquent before the observed inadequacies and injustices of their society. Someone must penetrate through the web of if's, options, and whereases, and state the issues in clear, monosyllabic honesty. "The American people," said Senator Edmund S. Muskie to the December, 1966, Third National Conference on Air Pollution, "do not care about the statistical analyses describing health effects from specific pollutants. But they do . . . want to be assured an adequate supply of breatheable, healthful air." So, too, and properly, the Christian will raise basic societal questions and will protest observed injustices. But somehow he must also be committed in those areas in which honest, if fallible, men wrestle to find answers and abolish social inequities. The Christian perspective must involve both viability and vision. It must include understanding of and participation in cybernetics, information and education, legislative processes, and working civic conferences. The Church which merely catalyzes protest and then absents itself from the tough task of finding the remedial how, when, and where stands culpable before man. Clearly this movement from a prophetic *no* will be to a constructive *yes*. It demands a patient presence. Former Vice-President Humphréy put it well in his address to the National Council of Churches:

What you have been doing [is] educating all of our citizens, arousing our conscience, pointing to social injustices . . . We are now in stage two of this wave of social reform—the tough, working stage of the follow through, when we find out how hard the job is, how long it will take, how much money it will cost, how many of our efforts need to be revised and improved.

It is a time when all too many crusaders are inclined to leave the march.[27]

He added, significantly sensing the role of voluntarism and government in society:

> There is one theory that puts government on one side, under a cloud of suspicion, and the action of private and voluntary groups on the other side, as purer, better, somehow more righteous and desirable. And there is the implication that governmental action and non-governmental action are competitive and that the more of the one the less of the other. But I suggest to you it isn't like that at all . . . Our pluralism is a source of strength. What is needed is a partnership in which our public and private institutions, working together, can meet public and private need without any one institution becoming a dominant monolith.

The Humphrey reasoning would seem to be that, as religion moves beyond a radical eloquence about injustice, it must more and more discover and operate through a working collection of officials and activists, all of whom are important and none of whom is totally good or totally bad. We have got to shoulder the wheel and push. We have got to join the fight as well as raise the banners. We must learn as well as love. Patrick Cardinal O'Boyle of Washington, D.C., put one aspect of this well:

> Religion alone can bring the inner, heart-felt recognition of the dignity of every man as a child of God. And when the religious forces of a community act as one, their moral impact is decisive.

---

[27]Address at Miami, Florida, December 7, 1966.

But moral principles must be implemented by concrete measures of civic life. To bring this about, religious leaders must be aided by those familiar with the social, political, and economic aspects of the problems we face. Hence we come to you, offering our assistance and friendship, but also asking you to inform and guide us. Without your help, and the counsel of many others who have worked long in the struggle for human rights, we could make serious mistakes. We could talk generalities that would have little impact on the heart-rending problems you know so well. We want to work with you, so that our efforts will be specific, concrete, and wisely conceived.[28]

To achieve a relevance at the vision and the viability levels, religious decision-makers need to consider these additional factors.

FIRST, normally the pattern of responsible institutional intervention in society is slow and progressive. Any institution which proposes to mold its milieu must reflect on itself in several dimensions. It must review and re-think its purpose and its principles. What is its world outlook? What do its documents, old and new, tell it about itself? What is its internal potential for effective intervention? It must next review and re-think the circumstances in which it exists. What is the precise situation in which it intervenes? What are the immediate crises? What are the consequences predictable from this as distinct from an alternative method of intervention in those crises? It must review and re-think its associational context. It has well been written: "The mere preaching of ideals or the offering of conscience-pricking

---

[28]Address to the Washington, D.C., Urban League, May 6, 1963.

criticisms will not be enough. The church that serves effectively in its community must join the team of groups, agencies, and individuals who strive for improvement in the community's welfare."[29] With what other institutions, agencies, and programs must the intervening religion work as it intervenes? What laws apply, what record of experience exists to guide it in its associational activity? Who and how are the key people involved? Once each of these initial self-reflections has been completed, normally two further deliberations and conclusions are required. The institution must structurally reform itself for a more mature intervention. Finally, it must deliberate and conclude as to particulars. Given these principles, these facts, this association, this structure, which proposals should it support, which reject? There is no question but what this is the most difficult of all the phases through which the intervening religion must pass. Pope John XXIII told the bishops of Latin America once that, while deliberation and freedom of judgment must prevail in a mature religion, there come times when the ranks of hierarchy and congregants must close on specific means toward agreed community ends. Knowledge of just when these times occur is extremely hard to come by. There is no simple formula, and the risk of reaction against specifics on two counts is great. On the one hand, the more an organization purporting to speak in the name of religion elects to proclaim a collective position, a particular stance on a problem with socio-political dimensions, the more likely the chance of dissension in its own membership. Dr. Eugene Carson Blake put it bluntly:

---

[29]Miller, p. 172.

The problem of the corporate church when it attempts to take relevant moral stands on real moral issues is very much the same as that of the individual preacher in his pulpit. Nobody complains if he keeps general enough. He will be applauded for general exhortations about love, generosity, peace, unselfishiness, and all the other Christian aims and virtues so long as he doesn't get down to cases. Nathan was in no trouble with King David until he said, "Thou art the man."[30]

On the other hand, the farther a religion removes itself from particulars, the less likely it is that it can make any lasting impact on the shape of things. All this, so far, has been a normal traditional précis of the institutional decision-making process. Admittedly, these are not normal times or normal cities. Still a similar, if abbreviated, analysis effort is urgent.

SECOND, increasingly, the city planner has learned two things. He has become ever more aware of the indivisibility of urban problems. He is increasingly conscious that he cannot begin to solve them all at once with equal effectiveness and that, even recognizing their wholeness, he must intervene in metropolis where and as he can partially. For the Christian, the learning experience of involvement in metropolis is the same. He becomes aware that all inequities simply cannot be removed at once. Nor can all good goals be perfectly achieved. Which problems, then, should he approach first? What priorities? How far must the responsible citizen compromise down from hundred percent solu-

---

[30]Eugene Carson Blake, Address at Colgate-Rochester Divinity School, April 18, 1960, as reported in *United States News and World Report*.

tions[31] in metropolis to get anything done at all? That decision, for the Christian, must be a factor, not only in determining the urgency of the particular problem, but also in determining his own and the community's capacity to solve it. Alvin Schorr calls poverty a "syndrome of reinforcing handicaps."[32] No simplistic remedy developed along one remedial line will suffice to relieve it. And this is true of many other issues in megalopolis. A systems approach, a continuing awareness of the interaction which produces the problems of society and must be built into their solution, is imperative. At the same time, and this will be hard for churchmen, we shall have to accept as involved persons something less than an ideal response to our civic sermons. Barbara Castle, British Minister of Transport, speaks of "the gorgeous irresponsibility of the expert." The outsider, the man who does not have to fund and compromise and locate, can be a dreamer. The insider, the official responsible to flesh-and-blood men and ground realities and limited moneys, must often give a little here and adjust a little there to get anything actually done. How do we in religion decide what the syndrome of handicaps and advantages in a particular case is, and then how do we move broadly in a real world to accommodate it? The decision is complicated by the fact that much more is involved than spiritual motivation

---

[31]I mean by this that when one approaches metropolis unilaterally, as housing, as parks, as schools, certain ideal patterns suggest themselves. There are standards in each area of concern which, if perfectly accommodated, would lead to solutions which would then become what I call one hundred percent solutions in that particular area of concern. Once these unilateral approaches are put together, as they must be, in the creation of a general plan, each must be adjusted into a total in which no single solution is any longer one hundred percent ideal.

[32]Alvin Schorr, *Slums and Social Insecurity*, Research Report #1 (Washington, D.C.; Department of Health, Education, and Welfare, 1965), p. 2.

and ideal hopes. Michael E. Schlitz points up the dilemma: "Very few concrete community situations present themselves in terms of clear-cut moral alternatives. Usually the choice in the community conflict is between alternatives and lies within the prudential, secular political dimension."[33] We shall also have to decide whether to accept the possible good in preference to the not immediately actionable better. John XXIII has suggested that we must not so lose ourselves in pursuit of ideals that we overlook what can be done here and now. Aristotle warns that the good is enemy to the best. What it comes down to, most probably, is steering between Scylla and Charybdis. We cannot be simply prisoners of a bureaucracy incapable of dreaming beyond immediate budgets and the inertia of office. Neither must we let ourselves run wild, dreaming too far outside the near possibility of human nature and ignoring what can be done here at this moment.

THIRD, whatever other refinements and requirements exist, a Christian seeking perspectives in metropolis must very soon discover that many of the key questions are rather ethical questions than questions of statistics and machinery. "The world cannot be saved from the outside."[34] Speaking on control of air pollution in Chicago recently, Northeast Illinois planner Matthew Rockwell titled his appeal for massive and costly action, "Do We Care Enough?" To the Urban American Conference in Washington, D.C., on 13 September 1966, former Vice-President Hubert H. Humph-

---

[33]Cf. *Commonweal* (March 25, 1966), p. 16.
[34]Paul VI in *Ecclesiam Suam*, August 6, 1964, NCWC edition, par. 87.

rey put simply what many others have observed: "We have the knowledge. We have the resources. And I believe we should have the wisdom to put them intelligently together. The critical question is this: Do we have the will?"

Man has an option in nuclear potential of moving toward the ultimate domination of the planet for his own happier habitation of it or blowing himself to cosmic dust in an ultimate catastrophe. He likewise has at least some form of limited option as to whether megalopolis moves down into parasitopolis and pathopolis or builds forward into a sanity in which both an equality of opportunity and a variety of choice co-exist. How do we as men of religion persuade him to will the bright rather than the dark urban option? But all this is the big, comprehensive choice. There are also dozens of local, specific choices which must be made. I have observed that one of the principal defects in human judgment is the inability of many citizens to add two and two and recognize a probable total of four. How do we further help to persuade man that doing certain things now in conjunction with certain other things will, whatever his announced objective, add up to certain results? This kind of inability to add is, especially, evident to planners. One of our first tasks in building a general plan for a community is to establish a self-consistency among the community's explicit and its subconscious goals. To do this we have to demonstrate that certain actions, as, for instance, extension of utilities into low density areas, produce certain other actions, as, for instance, increased subdivision activity. These actions have, therefore, to be estimated, not as isolated items, but as part of an overall interacting whole. So, too, the ethician in metropolis must demonstrate not only the rightness of great purposes but, and even more insistently, the cumulative morality of all those little decisions which combine to advance or retard such purposes.

FOURTH, one of the greatest urgencies in metropolis is for a working principle of common good. Few institutions in society are more insistently commanded to preach this principle than the Church. Few have a greater potential for doing so both with an enthusiastic human commitment and an objective detachment. Common good is a moral decision as much as it is tangible commonwealth; Jacques Maritain has written: "The common good is a different thing from the mere aggregation of particular goods . . . The common good is something ethically good."[35] Bishop John J. Wright of Pittsburgh in a major address on the subject repeated the Maritain theme: "A common good worthy of persons always presupposes a moral, intellectual, and spiritual element as essential and fundamental . . . A true common good must be a virtue, the virtue of persons acting with knowledge and consent."[36] One is reminded inevitably of the great Aquinian notion of participatory order, of intelligent beings sharing positively as well as receptively in their societal development. In *Pacem in Terris* John XXIII wrote: "Those, therefore, who claim their own rights, yet altogether forget or neglect to carry out their respective duties, are people who build with one hand and destroy with the other . . . The order which prevails in society is by nature moral."[37]

If this is true, then somehow commonwealth can be

---

[35]Jacques Maritain, *The Things That Are Not Caesar's* (London, 1930), p. 85.
[36]Address at Vatican II, November 28, 1964.
[37]*Pacem in Terris,* par. 30.

achieved in metropolis only when, in the words of Frank Lloyd Wright, enough citizens are activated by "the interior discipline of an ideal."[38] Common good is a matter of participation by an intelligent and concerned citizenry in the decisive processes as well as obedience to a decided law. Common good is not a matter of summit decisions imposed on a careless constituency which, until the moment of decision, is ethically free to engage in jungle warfare as among individual and collective selfishnesses. What is necessary is not static tyranny by the many over the few. Common good is not the consequence of stunting initiative and the instinct of self-preservation in some massive and inplacable objectification of values. It is not a question of a fallible me against a somehow wiser us. It is a question of presenting a citizen with the larger picture and convincing him that, when the whole improves, the part eventually shares in such improvement. Religion in metropolis must be particularly conscious of the difficulty as well as of the extreme importance of its role as catalyst and agent of the commonwealth. Its peculiar qualification, once it is itself informed, to speak of goals and translate means into understandable language is obvious.

The great historian of metropolis, Lewis Mumford, repeatedly details a critical role for religion in the city of our time. He writes, for instance, "The central position of the church or cathedral is the key to the layout of the medieval city . . . In fact one must think of the early church as what one would now call in America a community center."[39] The Calabrian monk Campanella dreamed and sketched an ideal

---

[38]Wright, p. 242.
[39]Mumford, pp. 54-55.

"city of the sun" in 1599. He centered it about a temple. The first communities in New England were also parishes. In Latin America church and cabildo were basic features of the central plaza. When Frank Lloyd Wright reversed himself (he had referred to the church as "the light that failed") to project his utopian Broadacre City around a cathedral, he said that in this kind of focal setting religion could "become again, and upon more noble social terms, the potent cultivator of independence, protector of the neighbor, pilot of human conscience, and thus alive for a whole people."[40] The Church will never again be medievally central to cities. But the Church can render a critically central civic service and, sometimes, even its structures begin to provide important nodes in urban renewal projects.

If we are indeed to fulfill this kind of community responsibility, religious decision-makers will require new testing, newly competent personnel, new structures, new thought, and new theologies of "the secular." All of this will need to start with the person of metropolitan man, but it cannot stop with this. It must become contextual, ecological in a sense, systematic. Architect Eliel Saarinen points this up simply: "Vitality in all life manifestation depends, first on the quality of the individual and, second, on the quality of the correlation."[41] If religion in metropolis must spark new commitments in personal concern for commonwealth, it must begin by recognizing that these commitments can become effective only in a multitude of interacting situations, constraints, moneys, and professionals, and in a context of newly alert citizens. It is simply not enough to command congregants to

[40]Wright, p. 203.
[41]Eliel Saarinen, *The City, Its Growth, Its Decay, Its Future* (Cambridge, Massachusetts: MIT Press Paperback, 1965), p. 9.

good citizenship. We have got somehow to associate ourselves with the processes of information and education, the
daily sweat of market and politics, understanding all along
that inter-disciplinariness is no longer the exception but the
very rule of metropolis. The forms of religion as civics must
be adjusted to reflect what an inter-disciplinary analysis
says to us about its functions.

To sum up, the job of phrasing a Christian perspective is
not easy. It is not simple. It is not singular. The job is
difficult, highly complex, continuous. Part of the complexity
arises from the fact that religion is a plural fact in metropolis. Its positive presence must, then, be developed in terms of
this pluralism. This will require both an internal effort in
each religious group and an external re-examination. Religion is only one of the many meliorative forces in metropolis. Its perspective will have to be applied in association
with other religious and non-religious agencies. It must bring
to this association new lights of comprehensive humanism
and practical love. It cannot do the job alone. Learning how
to think and work in such often shifting partnerships for
commonwealth will be one of the most important and
difficult facets of the entire planning operation.

One fundamental question remains to be asked. Can existing civic institutions and procedures be adapted to new
needs, or are massive, revolutionary-type changes required
in our society and our politics before we can equate our
theories to reality in metropolis? There are those who have
already opted for revolutionary change. For instance,

> The problems of a high school dropout cannot be understood
> without reference to the problems of schools. And the problems
> of the schools are reflections of the problems of the city. And
> the problems of the city are symptoms of the sickness of

society-at-large. Only a revolution, it seems, will solve the problems of a single high school dropout.[42]

I am sure that the situation is desperate. I am not sure it is so desperate. I suspect a reasonable analysis of the state of the nation must suggest that we try a little longer with institutions and professionals who themselves are changing before we opt for as yet indistinct substitutes. Unquestionably, though, what is required if systematic problems are to be solved is systematic solutions.

There are three further bench-marks which I believe are necessary for a mature Christian perspective in metropolis. First, religion must be more than a protest and terminal factor in social change. It must be continuous, competently comprehensive, and positive, as well as responding, local, and questioning. This will demand more of us than high hopes and pointing to problems from whose solution we then piously withdraw. Churchmen do well to listen to the counsel of the late Stephen R. Currier: "[You] must be more than harried respondents to urges and proposals that press upon [you. You] must become initiators and innovators with a key role in shaping the destiny of . . . people."[43]

Second, city planners have long since learned that they cannot shoot themselves to respect in metropolis. The planner must prove himself. Tacking his name in old English letters to a door or proclaiming platitudes about comprehensiveness will not suffice. Jesuit sociologist Joseph H.

---

[42]Gary Stallings, in "Renewal," Chicago Missionary Society (Christmas, 1966), p. 6.
[43]Address to Municipal Administrators at Urban America Conference, Washington, D.C., September 13, 1966.

Fichter has judged that "most churchmen—the decision-makers—are sociologically illiterate."[44] We have, in any case, passed well beyond what Franklin Littell calls the Constantinian era in which we were viceroys of a sacral state or, at least, we could count on a residual reverence where our voices were heard with a presumption of acceptance and in the dimensions of respect. Patiently as well as dramatically, in study as well as in street, thinking long distance as well as short, we shall have to establish our competence just as does any other professional. Only then can we begin to match our performance to our ideals for metropolitan man in this critically intricate society.

Third, the churches of metropolis must help lift the eyes of expert and citizen alike beyond the narrow, near horizons of what is immediately possible. They must become, in a sense, the out-riders of a radically better tomorrow. Joseph Turley, then executive director of Boston College's Boston Metropolitan Seminars, called them once "a platform on which advanced ideas can be presented." So, too, the Church is a challenge of hope. It must not, however, over-promise It must not so inspire man to ultimates that he neglects the here and now imperfect, but possible, remedies.

None of this, I suppose, is theology. Yet all of it is. The question is how the people of God can move from an aroused spirit to an effective involvement in a modern, metropolitan world. Vatican II said: ". . . by holding faithfully to the Gospel and benefiting from its resources, by joining with every man who loves and practices justice, Christians have

---

[44] Harvard Divinity School Colloquium on "Church and Synagogue in Boston Renewal," Cambridge, Masachusetts, January 30, 1964.

shouldered a gigantic task to be carried out in this world."
. . . *Constitution on the Church in the Modern World,*
paragraph 93.

Emmanuel Cardinal Suhard had written earlier: "We
cannot conceive of a spirituality abstracted from the contact
and influences of daily life, work, pleasures, housing, the
common opinion of friends, the outpourings of the cinema,
the press and the wireless. Sooner or later the problems of
reconciling life and spirituality arise."[45] Christopher Dawson
calls "the prophet . . . perhaps the greatest agent of social
change." Harvey Cox defines this kind of prophecy as including "discernment of the signs of the times, clarification
of moral options presented to human beings, and the sum-
moning of man to accountability in the light of the moral
traditions."[46] Hubert Humphrey wrote in his foreward to
Rabbi Richard Hirsch's *There Shall Be No Poor* (1965):
"Every significant social change in the history of America
has occurred because the conscience of the people was
aroused." It is in our conviction that these things are or, at
least, should be so that our perspective begins. We in the
religions of metropolis are called to prophecy and practice.
We are called to high ideals and immediate sweat. Can we
now by our demonstrated competence and our will to work
capture the conscience of metropolis and hold it?

---

[45]Abbe G. Michonneau, *Revolution in a City Parish* (Westminster,
Maryland: Newman Press, 1950), p. xiii.
[46]Cox, p. 7.

Metropolis

TWO

Technical civilization brings about not only changes in social values, not only new relationships between man and nature, but also changes in the relations between man and man in society. This is not just a minor change but, in a sense, a real mutation of mankind, and because we are just in the midst of it, it is so important that we become aware of what has happened, and what is in process of happening.[1]

The Christian, if indeed he has a message for metropolitan man, must express it through the medium of a real metropolis. The discovery and analysis of such reality is not easy. It requires as much concentration as is required to phrase a perspective and to begin to remake structures. Responsible intervention in metropolis must begin with responsible understanding of what and how metropolis is. The institution which proposes intelligently to help shape this phenomenon must: 1. be familiar with the qualitative

---

[1] Francois Houtart, *The Challenge to Change, The Church Confronts the Future* (New York: Sheed and Ward, 1964), p. 34.

and quantitative realities of change; 2. be aware of and equipped to participate in interaction between government, technology, and society; 3. operate in flexible association with a multitude of different professionals, politicians, and activists.

It is clear that a paramount fact in metropolis today is a revolution of instant expectations. This is succeeded often by a revolution of instant, massed, and at least pre-violent discontent. The relevant urban institution must face up to this reality. Two factors feed it. There is, first, a great yearning for and a new confidence in a one hundred per-cent solution to all our collective human problems. Thomas Molnar writes: "[the utopian adopts] the view that one single regeneration will take place, putting an end to history (that is, to the rule of chance and of the unpredictable) and ushering in a kind of timeless time, the last chapter in the Book of Man when everything will be settled, predictable, scientifically planned, and happy."[2]

As scientists increasingly celebrate our option over crea-tion, more and more of us become optimistic about new and sweeping urban uplift. At the same time, as the afflu-ence of so many becomes evident, the non-affluent are less and less willing to endure their observed inequality. The net result everywhere is a strident unwillingness to settle for slow or partial change. The urban institution today must operate against the backdrop of a chorus of substantive as well as technical questions, all of which are spoken with an insistence seldom before heard. Nor are these questions simply academic. The riots in Newark, Hough, and Watts

---

[2]Thomas Molnar, *Utopia, the Perennial Heresy* (New York: Sheed and Ward, 1967), p. 14.

are as much part of the urban situation in our time as informed debate in Congressional hearing rooms or graduate seminars. There is little prospect that we shall ever settle our cities in erudite conference or with dilatory Federal dollars alone.

Beyond this initial observation, the crisis in metropolis today is staggeringly great. Written into every metropolitan newspaper each day is evidence of a split urban personality. Metropolis is a schizophrenia of hope and hurt, new prospects and a continuing pathology of old inner and outer neuroses. There is crisis of cornfields turned into subdivisions. There is crisis in New York City the day after Thanksgiving, 1966, with its grey polluted skies. There is crisis in unsafe urban streets, crisis in prolific ghettoes, crisis in public welfare, and in the jumping cost of urban convenience. There is crisis as urban areas get bigger and the reach of the average citizen gets smaller. There is crisis in community action to repeal poverty.

What is required of the intervening institution is a clear appreciation of urban crises in both their large and their narrow dimensions.

It has been well suggested that the architect or planner who builds a three-dimensional model of a city and then simply looks down on it will never really come to understand that city. What is necessary is that he stoop and look through his model, taking a street-eye view, as the city's citizens see it every day. He must, in short, feel and breathe the community as well as number and map it. He must empathize with the ordinary city-dwellers, not just tabulate a steeple or top-of-city-hall outlook. So, too, in approaching metropolis: the churchman must stoop down and look through it. He has to become immediate and people-high, as well as engaging in long theories as to what might generally happen. If and as he does so, certain crises and certain programs stand out. They do not exhaust his metropolitan horizon. They do set dimensions within which a newly mature religious relevance must be activated.

Before and above all else there is in metropolis a crisis of people. There are at least three major aspects to this crisis. First, the benefits of urbanization have been unequally spread. William L. C. Wheaton, in a characterization now widely familiar, speaks of "two cultures":

> Roughly ¾ of our people have acquired the skills and resources to accept these [technological and societal] changes and benefit from them. The remaining fourth have never had the skills or resources, or are excluded from using them, and to them the urban revolution is calamitous. They are rapidly becoming the inheritance of our central cities.[3]

This difference, critical enough in itself, compounds itself along racial lines. While by no means all the non-affluent fourth of our people are Negro, most of those who live in metropolis are. In the decade 1950-1960, Negro non-affluence concentrated more than ever before in the American city. White population increased nine times as fast in the suburbs as in center city, but Negro population in all our standard metropolitan statistical areas increased seven times as fast in center city as in the suburbs. Whatever the reasons, the reality in metropolis is a mobile majority and a penned-up minority. As the revolution of rising white expectations sweeps out centrifugally from City Hall, the

---

[3]William L. C. Wheaton, cited in *The Intercollegian*, National Student Councils of the YMCA and YWCA, New York City (Spring, 1966), p. 15.

revolution of instant but still thwarted Negro expectations charges with newly explosive power through downtown. The relative fact of impressive Negro gains in the last decade seems insufficient to satisfy the continuing expectation. In fact, the National Advisory Commission on Civil Disorders in its February 29, 1968, summary wrote (chapter 12):

> Social and economic conditions in the riot cities constituted a clear pattern of severe disadvantage for Negroes compared with whites. . . . Negroes were twice as likely to be unemployed and three times as likely to be in unskilled and service jobs. Negroes averaged 70 per cent of the income earned by whites and were more than twice as likely to be living in poverty. [Negro] housing [was] . . . three times as likely to be overcrowded.

Second, the permanent vindication of human rights everywhere in metropolis will require massive wisdom as to the right tactics and the best procedures. After the Newark riots of July, 1967, HUD Secretary Robert C. Weaver warned that it was dangerously unreal to anticipate immediate and total urban change even with expanded Federal programs. HUD Undersecretary Robert C. Wood said at Catholic University on December 3, 1966, surveying the record of Federal activity in the city, that we have learned that "we must not overpromise." To excite hopes which cannot or cannot soon be fulfilled is a cruel hoax on the poor. It may set off volcanoes of frustration. Donald Caty, the editor of *Urban America,* has written:

> Every time something new whizzes way overhead or fizzles short of target, hope dies and frustration deepens. Yet, on the other hand, it must be more than business as usual in the

fight to remake our cities. Hopefully, a stepped up response
to urban need can be mounted without a succession of unrea-
soning turbulences. Hopefully the affluent and the near-afflu-
ent in our society will respond to the just demands of the poor
before blood is spilled in our streets or the threat of open
warfare in all our urban communities becomes too real to
ignore.[4]

One has only to re-read carefully the reporting on any
urban riot to appreciate the good and the bad which jostle
each other in neighborhood upheaval. Speaking of such
upheaval in his city, Mayor Hugh J. Addonizio of Newark
acknowledged: "Riots are in a great sense a convulsion, an
upheaval which at the bottom have people crying for help
and for consideration."[5] But he said those in Newark had
been "fueled by the rash of wild and extremist statements
and behavior of the past ten or twelve weeks in our city."[6]
Governor Richard Hughes called the Newark turmoil "a
criminal insurrection."[7] In his proclamation declaring a state
of emergency in Plainfield, New Jersey, issued on July 19,
1967, he pointed to these tragic consequences of street
anarchy:

> There presently exists . . . a state of disaster and emergency
> in which acts of homicide and violence, looting and burning
> are prevalent and . . . there have been serious injuries to
> persons and extensive damage destruction of property.[8]

Once again in comment on the riots of April, 1968, questions of outside agitators, imported weapons, the effective-

---

[4]Donald Cantz, "City" in *Urban America* (September, 1967), p. 2.
[5]*The New York Times* (July 19, 1967), p. 42.
[6]*Ibid.* (July 19, 1967), p. 1.
[7]*Ibid.* (July 20, 1967), p. 28.
[8]*Ibid.* (July 20, 1967), p. 28.

ness of existing welfare structures, police discretion, came sharply to the fore. Once again, answers were few and passions high. Does the urban institution work with or outside the "situation" it finds in the city? What stance ought religion adopt in the presence of the urban riot? It is quite true, as Rev. James P. Morton of the Urban Training Center in Chicago argues, "As prophet the Church can never be satisfied with what is, with what exists today. She hungers and thirsts for that new heaven and new earth now . . . and more, as prophet, the Church is confident that what exists today can be transformed."[9]

The difficulty arises, however, not in stating the urgency of deep-driving change, but in estimating the methods and timing of its achievement. The task of the Church is not only to shout justice but to sweat it into being with patience and perseverance. The task of the Church is also to ponder the whole picture, to look beyond the angry moment, to seek an accomplishment which will create a better pattern for tomorrow as well as solve today's here-and-now problem. The Church cannot ignore the riot, but more important are the urgencies of reform in the patterns and habits of civic response to the needs out of which riots arise. Prophecy is always dramatic and sometimes imperative, but unless the kind of prophecy which some call religion is coupled with a true appraisal of what is really potential about man and with a sophisticated awareness of its long-range impact on society, it could in our time be culpably imprudent. The difficulty, put in other words, is to decide what is indeed just. The record of community development in the American city is replete with evidences of the inability of even highly

---

[9]Address to the National League of Cities, Detroit, Michigan, July, 1965.

responsible men to decide what is right and what is wrong. In Newark, for instance, partly causative of the riot was the honest will of an honest mayor to keep a medical school downtown. Seldom has this critical uncertainty as between good goals and suggested alternatives to reach them been so devastatingly noticed as in Roger Starr's *The Living End.* He begins, "It all seems so easy, the issues so clear." He proceeds to spell out with telling accuracy the perplexity of city officials before "the conflicting demands of their citizens."[10] He annexes to this several wonderful paragraphs in which he points up the underlying controversies which wrack urban critics "in all respects but their assurance" that they are individually right. What emerges is a straight conclusion: cities are not simple; there is no universal agreement as to the means to obtain urban justice even if many of the goals of urban justice are almost as indisputable as "motherhood." It is all very well for the Church to hunger and thirst for justice in metropolis, but what the subsequent diet ought to be here and now in this city at this time remains at best controversial.

There have been a number of examples of such urban perplexity. One of the most striking was detailed a few years ago by two Columbia University professors of social work, Frances F. Piven and Richard A. Cloward. Usually, the cause of open housing and desegregation via Federal legislation and programming goes unchallenged in "progressive" circles. In their article in *The New Republic,* however, the two professors suggest that an open housing and desegregation clause may very seriously have impeded urban renewal and public housing programs. They write:

---

[10]Roger Starr, *The Living End: The City and Its Critics.* (New York: Coward-McCann, 1966), p. 23.

The Achilles heel of housing programs has been precisely our insistence that better housing for the black poor be achieved by residential desegregation. . . If group conflict is at the root of past failures, strategies must be found to improve ghetto housing without arousing the ire of powerful segments of the white community.[11]

Their proposed solution is clear: "The point, in short, is that if reformers can be persuaded to forfeit for a time the ideal of desegregation, there might be a chance of mustering political support and money for low-income housing."[12] I do not suggest that they are right. I do suggest that they point up a value conflict which is usual rather than rare in the urban decision process. I do suggest that, if indeed there is still time left to be reflective about methods, the question must again be raised of the presently impossible best *versus* the presently actionable good. The urban institution needs to ponder the method and fall out from mainstream and from street action to relieve poverty. The institution must come to grips with both types of remedial approach, must relate to the practitioners of each. It must recognize the perplexing gray areas in between. It has to be concerned for a total social system as well as for a particular challenge on a particular point. The sheer despair of the slum, the anomie and alienation of non-affluent urban neighborhoods have to be appreciated, empathized. Old ways will not do; one-to-one welfarism will not suffice. A Negro welfare worker in Plainfield, New Jersey, after Newark, remarked: "When these Negroes came, they thought Plainfield looked good compared with that they were used to, but now they no longer think it's so good. We aren't

---

[11]*The New Republic*, December 17, 1966, p. 27.
[12]*Ibid.*

doing anything to heal the basic dissatisfaction; all we do
is patching, a step here and there, but on the whole it's
depressing."[13]

It is often urged that only naked "power" will suffice,
that only street violence can adequately change things. But
is this really true? I am convinced that there is an upward
mobility in the conscience and mechanism of our society
which renders any easy dichotomy between do-nothing and
pre-violence (as if no alternative otherwise exists) untrue.
The legal and moral climates in which urban poverty survives have vastly altered since World War II. Landmark
Supreme Court decisions and Federal legislation have been
handed down. The key profession of social work shifts more
and more to a comprehensive, community-organization emphasis. Federal urban programs have moved increasingly to
a breadth which demands social as well as physical criteria
for success. Inevitably, too, volunteer welfare organizations
in any society reflect the conscience of that society. If the
conscience is mobile, so must the organization be, though
a time lag must be anticipated. All this combines to suggest
a third way to the intervening urban institutions. It is not
simply an old static establishment *versus* a new, brave
street revolution. Nor can the advocacy of naked "power"
as a means to the solution of urban problems be treated as
simply another manifestation of the old American custom
of rebelling against evil masters. As Mayor Thomas J. Whe-
lan of Jersey City, New Jersey, put it in his statement
before the Presidential Advisory Committee on Civil Disorders:

---

[13]*The New York Times* (July 20, 1967), p. 28.

Violence, rioting and racial conflict are nothing new in America. But in the past, rioting was generally directed against another group, while today's riots differ in that they are directed against all of society. . . There are groups in virtually every city who are working to bring about violence. . . We are dealing with a loose coalition of various elements under a string of common names, but all of whom have a common denominator. That common denominator is their hatred for our nation and its democratic institutions. In my view, they are, as Professor Moynihan of the Institute for Urban Affairs suggests, irreversibly committed to the destruction of American democratic society.[14]

Immediate gain through extreme polarization must be weighed against the activation of counter-forces and against the total long-range impact of such polarization on the community as a whole.

One of the key unanswered questions here is how fast we can move along this third way and whether we can do so in a manner adequately to meet the just demands of the urban non-affluent soon enough to avoid a resort to naked "power." After Detroit's riot of 1967, Walter Reuther said: "We were penalized by the fact that we had made great progress, but not sufficient progress."[15] The summer of 1967 did not suggest optimism, but perhaps the really important aspect is not the number of cities with riots, but rather the number of riotless cities in which constructive remedial action is underway.

The question of people in metropolis inescapably raises the question of ethics for metropolis. People have wills and

---

[14]Washington, D.C., October 5, 1967.
[15]Cf. *Urban America* (September, 1967), p. 2.

consciences. If metropolis is to be moved, it will first be moved through the wills and consciences of its citizens. There are already statistics, editorials, involved officials, concerned experts everywhere among us. What is mainly missing is metropolitan morality. There are simply not enough citizens in metropolis with an effective conviction that they have each a moral obligation to share in the burdens as well as enjoy the benefits of their metropolitan situation. Richard Cardinal Cushing of Boston put it well:

> At this moment we have the scientific knowledge, we have the material resources, we have the financial potential to eradicate the poverty that plagues our planet. What we do not have is the sense of urgency—the sense of impatience— the sense of optimism—the conviction that we can and must do it.[16]

In Utopia, Thomas More said, piety would be equated with a continuing preference for the common good over the single advantage. Aristotle and Thomas Aquinas both suggest that cities can be good only if the people in them are virtuous. Presumably the same thing is true of metropolis. But to what shall the metropolitan conscience commit itself? To high-density urban corridors and green wedges as in Copenhagen, or as in the Year 2000 Plan for Washington, D.C.? To the concept of girdling green belt with satellite new towns, as in London? To public housing projects blocked into otherwise affluent suburbs? To revived and newly magnetic downtowns somehow pulling urbanism back into a radial cohesion? To shining towers where there once

---

[16]In his pastoral letter, "The Servant Church," December, 1966, p. 19.

were expensive poor in the inner city? To folksy polyglot Jacobean neighborhoods? Or should the will and ethics of metropolitan man commit themselves rather to collective interaction in polynuclear urban areas in which expanding private leisure, moneys, and mobility roll each year farther out over the countryside? These, however, are the big options confronting the conscience of the metropolitan citizen, if indeed they are options at all. They are so big, in fact, that they stand well beyond the comprehension of the average citizen, much less his effective control. What really matters is the little, near options, the choices that over time add up to collective patterns. It is relatively easy, after all, to secure agreement on broad lines of social purpose. It is much less easy to find agreement on more specific means, as has been indicated above, or to convince people that doing this part of something here and now can, if repeated enough, develop into an important whole. Trouble, for instance, arose in one urban renewal area when the big objectives were spelled out in small and particular proposals:

> With the progress of the planning committee's work, the abstract generalized essentially vague goal of 'arresting blight,' restoring the former 'elegance and dignity,' *etc.*, was succeeded by very precise, detailed plans for the total area, specifying what might remain, what must not, what if it remained must be restored, rehabilitated, and the like.[17]

Once the generalities have been intemized into specific actions and the selected options begin to bite on individual

---

[17]Harold Goldblatt, *Citizen Participation in Urban Renewal* (Washington, D.C.: Health and Welfare Council of the National Capital Area, January, 1966), p. 66.

land and profits, the task of reaching concord is notably increased. Out of this kind of circumstance, the intervening church in metropolis must confront the question: What kind of moral advice, if any, should it provide the conscience of metropolitan man in the matter of particular options in community change? There has been much ambivalence in this area, some over-caution, perhaps, a good deal of bravado. Perhaps ambivalence is inevitable. But it does not help when the challenge is to build a positive policy for religious intervention in metropolitan decision-making. For instance, Karl Rahner, S.J., argues in one sentence for a freedom to diverge: "In principle there can in one and the same situation be several possibilities of action, not only practical but also justified."[18] In another, he suggests a need for unity: "It may be that in some given, temporary situation we have to stand together because of a radical threat to Christian and human values."[19] When does this latter moment of oneness arrive? Should the Church as institution in metropolis at times proclaim such a moment? Is religion justified—and if so, how often—in requiring its congregants and commanding society in general to support this rather than that metropolitan alternative as a matter of conscience? Is it possible to envision such a case arising in reference to a particular urban renewal project? And if it does not, are there then certain areas of metropolitan decision in which churchmen rightly intervene with regard to specifics and others in which they allow complete freedom to the individual conscience? On the other hand, if only a total freedom for

---

[18]Rev. Karl Rahner, S.J. *The Christian Commitment* (New York: Sheed and Ward, 1963), pp. 7, 8.
[19]*Ibid.*, p. 10.

individual option is desirable, does the Church remain forever in suspended judgment, merely proposing through its
press and its pastorals a number of options and then leaving
its congregants totally free to choose between them? Does
a pastor, to become local, merely poll his parishioners and
then throw his weight against or for specific civil proposi-
tions as the majority prefers; and if such a process is valid,
say, for a freeway, is it equally valid if those parishioners
reject integration in the parish environs? Where the question of taking a particular stand in a particular civic issue
arises, who has, if anyone, the right to bind a Christian
conscience? Has a bishop this right, and if so what superior
understanding of complex civic situations does consecration
confer upon him? If the bishop has no such right, then who
else does? And if no one does, is every Catholic who, with
a subjectively satisfied conscience, takes a stand for or
against a particular civic proposal equally justified? Is
there perhaps no place for conscience direction in metropolitan change? Ought the matter be left entirely free so
far as the intervention is concerned?

The issue is not whether one chooses to live out or in.
The debate over centering in or de-centering from "cities"
may be useful for academic entertainment. It may even in
practice have financial and psychological aspects. It is not,
however, a matter of ethics nor predictably a matter which
can be resolved by willing it one way or the other. Man
exists neither for city nor for suburb nor, for that matter,
for farm. He has no obligation to settle down in any one
place, close in or far out or middling. What is important is
that wherever he elects to locate, he must recognize the
increasing interdependence of all the parts and persons of
metropolis. What is important is that he acknowledge this

interdependence even when it requires personal inconvenience and some immediate self-sacrifice. Religion, too, has no obligation to any place or jurisdiction any more than it has to any form of government. Religion in metropolis is committed only to the common good of people. This today is emphatically a metropolitan good. The challenge to deal with the crisis of people in metropolis is a challenge to promote metropolitan citizen responsibility. It is not helped by trench warfare as between parochial cities and parochial suburbs. It is not helped by pretending that America is still simply "urban" and "rural."

In proposing such a metropolitan citizenship, however, a further difficulty arises. Citizenship for what? We can't agree on common good in a single community. How can we agree when the issue spans many communities? Again, as we have done so often through history, we shall perhaps have to back into commonwealth by way of enlightened self-interest, by way of self-defense against common evils. These latter range in metropolis from polluted environment, traffic strangulation, unequal educational opportunities, housing bias to inadequate job chances. In *Goals for Americans,* a grim tabulation of these evils is made:

> The social costs of the metropolitan environment are evident: the purgatory of the in-migrants, racial conflict, juvenile delinquency, the dreary lives of the aged, traffic congestion, the lengthening journey to work, the services that never catch up with the need, slums, and the chronic shortage of decent, moderate-priced housing, smog, crowded schools, ugliness and noise in the center, monotony and inconvenience in the suburbs.[20]

---

[20]*Goals for America* (Englewood Cliffs, N.J.: Prentice-Hall, Spectrum Book, 1960), p. 227.

Boston's former renewal chief, Edward J. Logue, saw in New York City an "enormous misery in which more than a million people spend their lives."[21] Not every common evil is so obvious, but there are enough obvious ones to begin to marshal a remedial and preventive common will against them. In short, the crisis of people in metropolis is one of little citizens challenged by giant problems, of a grinding disparity in material and psychological achievement and of problems unsolved because not enough people care enough to want to solve them. In such a crisis, the urgency for competent intermediaries between public need and private responsibility is obvious.

There is also in metropolis a *crisis of government*. Vertically and horizontally, public agencies and public programs multiply across the land. Neither experience nor study can tell us yet if this crisis can be solved through a form of metropolitan government. Some suspect that we shall simply continue linking ourselves in service accommodations while the power remains, at least in appearance, local. In any case, one of the most significant characteristics of Federal action in metropolis has been precisely a push toward a real comprehensiveness. It is happening in transportation; it is supposed to be happening in planning; it is inevitable in pollution control efforts. One commentator notes: "Having for long acted piecemeal through a variety of state and local unifunctional agencies, the federal government has come to realize the importance of overall local coordination if its resources are to have their desired effect."[22] The net

[21]*Let There Be Commitment* (New York: Institute of Public Administration, 1966), p. 1.

[22]Morton E. Long, in *Urban Research and Policy Planning, Volume I, Urban Affairs Annual Review,* edited by Schnore and Fagin (Beverly Hills, California: Sage Publications, 1967), p. 255.

result is still far short of an organized metropolis-wide structure of control and relation. Even in Toronto, the longest North American experience with such a structure, the record of success is not yet final enough for normative judgment. Councils of government, however, are new key words in the vocabulary of metropolis, and the requirements of service efficiency plus Federal grant-in-aid criteria combine to create at least an operating regionalism at many points. "The critical issue today," said *Goals for America* "is how to guide the future organization of the metropolis."[23] Again the urgency for intermediaries who will note the need and help prepare the public will to accept it is obvious.

There is *a crisis of movement*. How to express the new and vastly more diverse needs and habits of daily movement through metropolis, without destroying other goods, is one of the most difficult of our urban tasks. Origin and desire lines have broken forever free of old radial roots. The journey to work lengthens and diversifies. As people more and more live elsewhere than central, so jobs, fun, shopping, and schools themslves shift off center. The automobile, resented and cursed in the abstract, becomes increasingly indispensable in the particular. Public transportation remains a perplexing uncertainty, despite successes here and there after massive expenditure. Huge areas of our cities lie dead under blankets of asphalt and concrete, with parking meters standing like crosses on the grave. The interstate system, plus fast-growing miles of circumferential highway, make it easier to get out of as well as into our cities and easier still to avoid downtown altogether. Citizens in city after city zero in on freeways as symbols of what

[23]*Goals for America,* p. 228.

they consider aggression by things on people. In short, the crisis of movement grows geometrically as metropolis itself widens. There is every prospect that more leisure, more money, more mobility will make ease of movement through longer distances even more imperative in metropolis and at the same time even more difficult. Once more, the responsibly intervening urban institution will discover an important intermediary role as between the problem and the people.

There is *a crisis of waste*. It has well been noted that there are two things which man has never been able to do. He has not abolished war. He has not yet figured a way effectively to handle his own waste. Alvin M. Weinberg speaks of "the increasingly serious physical insults to the biosphere imposed by our industrial civilization."[24]

Increasingly, the dangers of air and water pollution multiply. Air and water management require a syndrome of reinforcing incentives, penalties, and controls. Land-use decisions, automotive reform, power shifts in industrial plants, new methods of municipal and private incineration—all these must be encompassed in a sustained combination of technology and law if metropolis is to be habitable. We have made very important beginnings toward comprehensiveness in this critical area. The National Conference on Air Pollution in Washington in December, 1966, was indicative of this. The question remains as to how far we will bend our single and collective wills to the expense and the restriction which effective waste management requires. Here, again, the relevant urban institution can play a key inspirational influence. In my comments to the final Plenary

[24]Alvin Weinberg, *Reflections on Big Science* (Cambridge, Massachusetts: Massachusetts Institute of Technology Press, 1967), p. 30.

Session of the Conference on December 14, 1966, I put it this way:

> The American people are activated in this critical area, as in so many others, by a new social conscience. They now rise to defeat the menace of polluted air. The nation will simply no longer submit to this short-changing of its right to environmental decency . . . To assist in this catalysis of new citizen involvement, the middle leadership levels of society are challenged to action. These are universities, churches, labor, business and farm organizations. Air pollution should stand high on their continuing agenda and should be featured in all their urban affairs conferences. For example, the churches of the nation should become as committed to the fight for the human right of clean air as some of them have been committed to the fight for other civil rights.[25]

This is not an exhaustive disjunction of crises in metropolis, yet it is perhaps sufficient to indicate a valid context of size and complexity. The sheer dimensions of such crises must not, however, blind us to the near details. Societal problems break down into millions of single problems. As the vicar of a London parish put it:

> It is clear to me that we shall be involved in more than what is usually considered as the problem of housing . . . The problems, of course, are more than local . . . They cannot be solved at the level of the parish . . . But it may be some contribution to make if a parish priest is never able to forget that a statistic like 'there is probably still a national shortage of 750,000 to a million houses, possibly more' must be interpreted in terms of human misery, in terms of family

---

[25]*Conference Proceedings* (Washington, D.C.: Health, Education and Welfare, 1967), p. 622.

breakdown and of psychological damage inflicted through over-crowding.[26]

All of these private hurts and hopes are, as never before, structured into social inadequacies. All of these private hurts and hopes have been, as it were, socialized to the point where only a massive socialization of remedies can heal them and keep them healed. Roger Starr has written: "The attempt to reconcile the mass and the individual cannot succeed perfectly from any position on the common ground. Effective planning is impossible until planners recognize once again that the collective will stands on a moral pinnacle at least as high as that of the individual."[27] People and automobiles, people and subways, people and public housing, people and parks—the list is long—these are clearly parts of a continuum, a continuity of action, not polar opposites. The urban institution, as it listens to public debate in metropolis, must not be trapped into fighting proposals which will, over a period of time, advance the good of the entire community, simply because they have an immediately negative social impact on one section of that community. Given a reasonable recognition and accommodation of its side effects, a proposal which improves metropolis anywhere in some major measure must, in time, lift the lives of people in metropolis everywhere. At least this has to be the rationale for planning. Nothing would ever occur in our cities if we had to wait to do it until each single sector of the community agreed to it and it did not here and now hurt any-

---

[26]Rev. Eric James, in *Town and Country Planning Review* (University of Liverpool, October, 1960), p. 343.
[27]*Planning 1966*, ASPO, p. 133.

where. It is, of course, wholly right to question priorities of need and feasibility. All this, however, is quite different from validating a division of programs for metropolis on a for-or-against-people basis. Few things should be more quickly spotted by the intervening metropolitan institution than prejudice or unfairness or lack of proper human concern in any planned project. Few things should be resisted more strongly by the intervening metropolitan institution that the raising of suspicions of injustice when in fact they are not sustained by the facts of the case. Indeed, just as churches ought to jump to the rostrums first to protest decisions which fail to account for just human claims on metropolis, so churchmen ought to jump to the rostrums first to denounce rumor-spreaders who seek to defeat a particular project in community development by raising charges of prejudice or racism or such like when, in fact, no such charge is justified by the situation.

There are three principal urban programs which need to be assessed:

I. URBAN RENEWAL. The Housing Act of 1949 proclaimed as a national purpose "the realization as soon as feasible of the goal of a decent home and a suitable living environment for every American family." The same act enabled urban redevelopment. This was a first effort to move coherently against slums. Shortly after his inauguration in January, 1953, President Eisenhower created an Advisory Committee on Government Housing Policies. The Committee reported on November 14, 1953:

The program must be closely integrated, comprehensive, and meet the twin objectives of satisfying the demand of the American people for good homes and the maintenance of a sound and growing economy . . . A piecemeal attack on slums simply will not work—occasional thrusts at slum pockets in one section of a city will only push slums to other sections unless an effective program exists for attacking the entire problem of urban decay.

In the light of this report, the Housing Act of 1954 replaced urban redevelopment with urban renewal. Conservation and rehabilitation were added to urban redevelopment's clearance methodology. A workable program was required. This was designed to demonstrate that a community was administratively, fiscally, and operationally ready for a comprehensive attack on blight. Public housing was to be closely related to renewal. As of December 31, 1966, 1,268 urban renewal projects had been approved for execution and 544 were in the planning stage. Eight hundred and forty-six American communities were involved in renewal activity.[28]

Real estate man Robert Futterman said once that the American city is "alternating bands of glory and garbage."[29] So, too, city renewal has run into alternating moments of glory and garbage. It has been saluted as seminal inspiration, seed money. It has been denounced as unconstitutional, "Negro removal," a gravy train for developers. One thing at least is obvious. Urban renewal cut away the facade which had hidden the problem of cities. It exposed for all to see the almost incredible intricacy of slums. This has had its salutary but also its negative, impact on the urban renewal record.

---

[28]*Housing and Urban Development*, SOR #30, December 31, 1966.
[29]Robert Futterman, *Future of Our Cities* (New York: Doubleday, 1961), p. 27.

It may be that much of the animus directed against urban renewal is an angry reaction to the sordid realities of American society which the program has exposed. For it is new evidence that curing these social ills is essential to the rebuilding of our cities.[30]

The argument over the success or failure of urban renewal has now moved well back stage as model-cities efforts and the war on poverty move up center stage. Renewal can no longer be estimated as the single principal Federal urban program. It must now be judged in conjunction with many other programs using many devices new and old to eliminate urban disadvantages. The key word, in fact, in metropolis programming is innovative. Still renewal remains a major part of the disjunction. Judgment of it continues important.

As in so many urban controversies, a lot depends on where one sits, one's criteria for analysis, and what one chooses to notice. Here, too, the observer tints the observed. Here, too, there is politics in research. Urban renewal should neither be faulted for not having done everything that needs doing downtown, nor praised for having accomplished more than it did accomplish. Former Secretary Weaver sums up the case for renewal:

Urban renewal can claim credit for a number of "solid accomplishments. . . . In scores of cities new communities of attractive housing, impressive public buildings, commercial structures, and industrial developments have been built. Numbers aside, perhaps the major achievement of urban renewal is that it has restored hope for older cities and

---

[30]Joseph Epstein, in *Harper's* (February, 1965), p. 61.

worn out neighborhoods, providing local leaders and gov-
ernments the tools for revitalizing their communities."[31]
This new and viable hope has been placed in a context of
comprehensive assessment of the city's potential and need.
Like any other urban effort, renewal has learned by doing.
More and more it talks social. Renewal, too, has been structured around a combination of public moneys and private
investment. If the end purpose of public decision can be
achieved through such a combination, surely this method
is preferable to straight municipal action. Finally, while
renewal has not been able totally to remake cities, it has
focused notice on particular problem areas and, in starting
to improve these, has demonstrated what can be done. Mrs.
Jane Jacobs calls renewal money "cataclysmic," but only
through such giant expenditure can the American city
seriously change itself. This, at least, is how the leading
arguments for renewal run.

On the other side, there are continuing questions as to
whether renewal has indeed reached the high goals set for
it in enabling legislation. Martin Anderson, in his now
classic *The Federal Bulldozer,* is blunt:

> Hundreds of thousands of people have been forcibly evicted
> from their homes in the past and it will not be long before
> the number passes the million mark. The indications are that
> these people have not been helped in any significant way.
> Their incomes remain the same; they are still discriminated
> against; and their social characteristics remain essentially
> unchanged. It appears that the federal urban renewal pro-
> gram has not achieved its social objectives to any measurable

---

[31]Robert C. Weaver, *The Urban Complex* (New York: Doubleday, 1964),
pp. 95, 96.

extent in the past; and if the program continues in the same pattern, it is unlikely that it will achieve them in the future. On balance, the federal urban renewal program has accomplished little in the past and it appears doubtful if it will accomplish much in the future.[32]

Charles Abrams has said: "This urban renewal program, while it does help cities get rid of slums, has developed into a device for displacing the poor from their footholds to make way for higher rental dwellings which those displaced cannot afford."[33] Sharp debate centers around the relocation of families displaced by renewal. Chester Hartman, after a long study of "The Housing of Relocated Families," concludes:

> Given the premise that one of the cardinal aims of renewal and rehousing should be the improved housing welfare of those living in substandard conditions, it is questionable whether the limited and inconsistent gains reported in most studies represent an acceptable level of achievement. Not only have the gains been limited, but they have been accompanied by widespread increases in housing costs, often incurred irrespective of an improvement in housing or the ability or desire to absorb these costs . . . It is an inescapable conclusion that relocation has been only an ancillary component of the renewal process.[34]

Citizen involvement in renewal is a moot point. In my study of Southwest Washington's pioneer urban renewal

---

[32]Martin Anderson, *The Federal Bulldozer* (Cambridge, Massachusetts: McGraw-Hill Paperback, MIT Press, 1967), p. 230.
[33]Charles Abrams, testimony before the Senate Committee on Banking and Currency, Washington, D.C., May 14, 1959.
[34]Chester Hartman, "The Housing of Relocated Families" in *AIP Journal* (November, 1964), p. 275.

effort,[35] I had to wonder whether honest and responsible dissent from the fast-changing renewal plans of the Redevelopment Land Agency had indeed been fairly accommodated. Increasingly, as renewal shifts into larger components of non-residential activity, questions arise as to its utility as a social welfare program. Yet, critics claim, and I believe they are right, that this was very clearly the intention of the Congress when it wrote the Housing Act of 1954.

Urban renewal marches on to cheers and jeers. If it is far too soon to say how it will fit into the new patterns of Federal urban effort, it is not too soon to suggest one or two questions which the intervening urban institution will want to direct toward its renewers:

1. Somewhere along the renewal line, if not in the first or second project, at least in the third or fourth, is realistic and firm provision being made for housing in the lower-middle income category?

2. Is citizen participation merely a matter of letterhead VIP committees who grandiloquently approve what has already been decided, with no real substance to it? Even admitting that much of such participation can be unreasonably negative, when it is responsibly critical, is this criticism courteously received and, where feasible, accommodated?

3. Are "social" planners, for instance, neighborhood settlement house and community services personnel, being involved in a real partnership for renewal? Are they free to speak out frankly? On the other hand, when they do speak, are they realistic about what can be done? How

---

[35]*Crisis Downtown* (Washington, D.C.: National Conference of Catholic Charities, 1959).

valid are the renewer's frequent responses that such and such a proposal cannot in the present state of things in the community be activated?

4. Given massive evidence that relocation has been a key problem in urban renewal to date, is a consistently detailed and frank attention being directed toward it? Or, while eliminating one slum, are other slums multiplied with citizen attention diverted from a real human need in a kind of urban sleight of hand?

II. PUBLIC HOUSING. Here, too, we deal with a controversial record. There can be little real doubt as to the need. There is much perplexity as to the means and the speed of action to meet that need. Since President Franklin D. Roosevelt signed the United States Housing Act on September 1, 1937, some 650,000 units of public housing have been built in this country. Most have been large, rectangular, high-rise blocks; some have been low-rise row housing; a few have been individual units in nonpublic housing neighborhoods. Most have been stuck like giant undigested bulks in the craw of cities. From the start the public housing effort has been seriously impeded by what Marie C. Maguire, whom President Kennedy named Commissioner of the Public Housing Administration in 1961, calls "a reluctant Congress, a sniping opposition, a cautious Administration, an uninformed public."[36]

In recent years, these indigenous difficulties of the effort have been much compounded: urban renewal and a notably expanded highway program required a massive receptacle

---

[36]Marie C. Maguire, in *Journal of Housing* (Washington, D.C.: National Association of Housing and Redevelopment Officials, October, 1962), p. 430.

in which hundreds of displaced families could be accommodated. There have been almost continuous debates as to public housing architecture, as to what is or is not a dispensable "frill," as to entry and exit income levels. Again and again, a minimal Congressional commitment cut back the hopes of public housing administrators. Again and again, the program has been bogged down with agonizing questions of class, color, and location. Even today it is estimated that only 27 percent of the nation's public housing projects are integrated. Again and again, projects have been attacked as high-rise ghettoes in which problems and problem families collect and which are as inescapably derogatory of the urban scene as of the urban soul. The plea for scatteration of housing projects through suburbia, like the plea for small units tastefully mixed with private housing, has come smack up against neighborhood resistance and the sheer urgency of quick, large housing resources to accommodate mounting public disclocations.

Many varieties of solutions have been advanced to meet these problems. None has yet proven fully effective. Meanwhile, public housing in metropolis remains in a quandary. There are, however, these hopeful signs. The intervening urban institution should cooperate actively in further development of each.

1. There is a growing awareness of the need for excellence in housing design. If for no other reason than that they simply do not accord with the image of a shining new city, the likelihood is that at least the shell of public housing will be up-graded.

2. There is a growing awareness of the need for comprehensive social services as well as for a decent physical

situation if the residents of public housing are to be helped into self-improvement. These services, it is recognized, must be located either in the projects themselves or near to them.

3. There are major efforts already underway toward innovative breakthroughs in rehabilitation of existing housing for public tenancy.

4. The likelihood is that, as other urban programs demand a participatory poor, tenant involvement in public housing, self-improvement will increase.

III. MODEL NEIGHBORHOODS IN DEMONSTRATION CITIES. On March 2, 1965, President Lyndon Johnson suggested to the Congress the urgency of an even wider perspective on urban problems than was possible under existing legislation: "To build not just housing units, but neighborhoods, not just to construct schools, but to educate children, not just to raise income, but to create beauty, and end the poisoning of our environment." On January 26, 1966, he called for a structured approach to total urban problems through a Model Cities effort. This, he said, would have to move out beyond existing frontiers. "Let there be debate over means and priorities. Let there be experiment with a dozen approaches or a hundred. But let there be commitment. . . . I propose that we focus all the techniques and talents within our society on the civics of the American city." This urgency resulted in passage of the Demonstration Cities and Metropolitan Development Act of 1966. Among other things, Title I of the Act provided: "Generally to improve living conditions for the people who live in such (i.e., slum) areas, and to accomplish these objectives through the most effective and economical concentration and coordination of federal, state and local public and private efforts to improve the quality of urban life." Of the total cost of planning and developing comprehensive city demonstration programs 80 percent will be borne by the Federal government. Communities of all sizes, singly and jointly, are eligible. In its instruction for application (*Improving the Quality of Urban Life*, HUD, 12 January, 1967), the Department of Housing and Urban Development identifies a model neighborhood:

> The model neighborhood area should be predominantly residential in character. Commercial and industrial areas of the city should not be included except as they are directly and primarily related to the needs of the people of the neighborhood for services or for jobs. Areas selected . . . should be at least in part hard-core slums. . . . The overall emphasis . . . is on rehabilitation.

To receive funds, the instruction continues, a community must prove:

1. that it has adequately identified and analyzed the economic, physical, and social problems in the proposed model neighborhood;

2. that it has begun to develop "high but realizable" goals, expressed wherever feasible quantitatively with at least an initial five-year-time dimension;

3. that it has created a system of programs and strategies which is "innovative," that is, substantially beyond its current level of urban action, and "comprehensive";

4. that an administrative mechanism adequate to the need envisioned has been or will be created and that this mechanism will make "the fullest utilization . . . of private initiative and enterprise," assure "widespread citizen participation," and provide "maximum opportunities for employing

residents of the area in all phases." Generally, the instruction warns, the City Demonstration Agency "should not be a special purpose agency with an independent governing board which is not representative of major agencies and interests involved in the program."

H. Ralph Taylor, HUD's Assistant Secretary for Demonstrations and Inter-Governmental Relations, suggests that the program must "substantially improve the living environment of people living in slums [through] . . . a coordinated attack."[73] He says it requires a change in people, a change in institutions and development of the economy. The Act indicates that tactics to be adapted toward these great ends include:

1. planning and execution of locally prepared and scheduled comprehensive city demonstration programs with boldly innovative ideas;

2. expansion of housing, job, and income opportunities;

3. reduction of dependence on welfare payments;

4. improvement of educational facilities and programs;

5. establishment of better access between homes and jobs.

It is, of course, far too soon to judge the impact of the Model Neighborhoods effort. Moneys have just recently been allocated. The total appropriation is small. There is some skepticism that, for all the talk about innovation, the program will be simply more of methods which have so far proved inadequate. If action can be suited to words, however, and a sufficient fiscal resource provided, the program could become a major break-through to new comprehensive urban

---

[37]H. Ralph Taylor, in *Model Neighborhoods under the Demonstration Cities Act* (HUD, 1967), p. i.

sense as cities compete with cities to discover and communicate working ideas and models for renewal. At the very least, unlike urban renewal, it emerges in a nation somewhat more habituated to urban comprehensiveness, somewhat more sensitive in its urban conscience. James E. Webb, President of the American Society for Public Administration, says: "There can remain little doubt that our society has resolved to undertake a great experiment, that we have set the goal of creating an urban society where all of our citizens can participate fully.[38]

This, then, is the board on which the relevant Church must play its urban game: a "crisis" says *Urban America* "of people, slum-ghettos, money, and power"; a congestion of programs, high and wide hopes, professionals and perplexed citizens!

In 1954, the title of Washington, D.C.'s first workable program was "No Slums in Ten Years." Progress has been made since that time, but slums in great and spreading chunks remain. Twenty years almost after the monumental Housing Act of 1949, we have still not really discovered the answers to metropolitan disorder and urban inequity. That is not, of course, the principal point, even if it is a point which cannot be ignored. The real point is that we have been trying, many of us, honestly, in many places. The real point is that we stand closer, for all our obvious failures, to success than we were before.

Surely, former President Johnson was right when he recalled the nation's many urban programs at his press conference after Newark:

---

[38]*Monograph #7, Annals of the American Academy of Political and Social Science* (Philadelphia, Pennsylvania, May, 1967), p. xi.

All of these things have not remedied the situation that exists. Until we can improve and correct them, we are going to be confronted with unpleasant situations . . . They [the riots] emphasize the necessity of the people of this country realizing that we must get on with the job of improving living conditions, educational and employment opportunities where people are—and they are in the cities. We can't correct it overnight. We can't correct it in a day or a year or a decade. But we are trying at this end of the line as best we can.

Our task as churchmen in this mixture of a low achievement and increasingly wise programming is both difficult and insistent. Its difficulty and the urgency of it multiply as we move into former Vice-President Humphrey's second phase of social reform. We must first understand what it is which stretches on all sides of us as we look from our steeples for a citizen's eye-view of metropolis. We shall have to point bravely but feasibly north—speaking to the doers, the movers and the shakers, the money men, the planners. In Frank Lloyd Wright's book *The Living City*, there is a picture of the concrete canyons of Big City, USA, taken from the air through a sea of smog. Its caption reads, "Find the Citizen!" Most of all, our task is to find the citizen and give him a real role on the urban board.

For one of the key goals in "citizen participation" is to reduce "the psychic distance among the participants"[39] in the urban game. Our role as bridgers and motivators in society is thus a critical role when it comes to involving citizens in community development.

We must also face up to several questions as we move

[39]*New York City Renewal Strategy*, (New York City Planning Commission, December, 1965), p. 8.

from recognition of role to accomplishment of it. How shall we deal with the schizophrenia which seems to emerge from the societal views of a man like Marshall McLuhan? On the other hand, he sees the individual citizen as continuously activated by cool media and bombarded by the information explosion. The net effect is to involve that citizen "in the whole of mankind . . . and the whole of mankind in"[40] him. On the other hand, galloping automation eliminates the need for a great deal of hackwork. And yet it is in the daily pedestrian hackwork of society that decisions and policies begin. The individual citizen tends to collapse into specialism which tends further to reduce his collective social conscience. Finally, the staggering impact of things, theories, and over-information can produce a numbing apathy. As McLuhan says, "The price of eternal vigilance is indifference."[41] What effect on local-citizen participation will the principle of sub-sidiarity have as it is operating to remove more and more issues to Federal control and away from local places and people? Are we possibly approaching the day when citizen participation for all the noble proclamations will consist mainly in choosing between increasingly sophisticated spare-time options and otherwise now and then throwing collective monkey wrenches into normally perfect civic machines? However such dilemmas are resolved, the role of religion in activating reasonable citizens in metropolis is clear. We must, as best we can, join hands with public and private agencies to help sketch out for the community certain ac-tionable options, large and small, to question responsibly the

---

[40]Marshall McLuhan, *Understanding Media* (New York: McGraw-Hill, 1964).
 [41]*Ibid.*, p. 43.

adequacy of present solutions, and to work with citizens in high and low places toward new solutions. And all of this has to be thought through in terms of two realities: first, the inescapable presence of a justly impatient poor; second, a realization that citizenship in the democracy today requires both courage and humility.

A decade ago the Rockefeller Panel on "Prospects for America" posed the twin requirement for such citizenship in this excellent insight:

> The ideal citizen of a democracy has enough spirit to question the decisions of his leaders and enough sense of responsibility to let decisions be made. He has enough pride to refuse to be awed by authority and enough humility to recognize that he too is limited in knowledge and in the power to be perfectly disinterested.[42]

At the same time, we shall have to ponder with the experts what revolutions in science and technology tell metropolitan man about his future. Alvin M. Weinberg, Director of the Oak Ridge National Laboratory, lists these revolutions as follows: "The thermodynamic revolutions . . . The nuclear-energy revolution . . . revolution in information. . . ."[43] What, in time, will cheap, portable energy do to people in cities? How will urbanism emerge from its encounter with the peaceful atom? Will, indeed, the computer "shine as a powerful instrument for making business more creative and efficient and, hence, for raising the Nation's real income per person, for eliminating an unlimited amount of drudgery,

---

[42]*Prospects for America*, pp. 405, 406.
[43]Alvin M. Weinberg, *Reflections on Big Science*.

and for increasing leisure, in short, for measurably expanding free man's range of choices?"[44]

I believe we in religion can rise to meet these and other new metropolitan challenges to our moral judgment. We have, indeed, no alternative but to try. I am equally sure that to do so will require of us a greatly expanded, continuous effort, marshalling all our resources in study as well as in empathy, in sweat as well as in prophecy. The important thing is really not whether the city is secular or not, or whether metropolitan man listens to us for our reasons or not, but simply whether out of our inner strengths and special empathies we come to him with helpful hope and hopeful help.

Perhaps nothing is more evident as we view metropolis today than that technology is not in itself enough. Somehow the mind and heart and will of metropolitan man must be newly shaped to meet the societal problems which survive into his contemporary metropolis. He will be mightily helped by his machines, but he remains the decision-maker.

H. Wentworth Eldredge put the case well when he wrote: "There are not going to be any new and shining cities without new and shining people in some as yet not entirely clear reciprocal relationship."[45]

Nor can the lesson of EXPO'67 be avoided. In opening it on April 27, 1967, Mayor Jean Drapeau of Montreal called it "the image and idea of a fraternal world, a united, peaceful welcoming world . . . a sanctuary . . . an exchange of ideas,

---

[44]C. L. Allen, Oak Ridge National Laboratories to Workshop on Science for Clergymen, Oak Ridge, Tennessee, August 8, 1967.
[45]H. Wentworth Eldredge, in *Taming Megalopolis*, Vol. 1 (Garden City, New York: Doubleday, 1967), Anchor Books, pp. vii, viii.

a meeting of minds, mutual understanding, love and peace."
Yet even during its magnificent mandate to a harmony
based on technology and communication, there was flaming
discord in the Middle East, death in the green hills of Viet-
nam, riots in Newark and Detroit, and the incident De
Gaulle. In its time context, then, the message of 1967 and
EXPO was one of much hope and great potential, but also
of surviving frustration, of the reach of the mind and machines of man, yet still of a fundamental flaw in him which
some will call orneriness, some sin, some aggression, and
many just plain selfishness. In short, the major message of
metropolis as medium today is at once technical and ethical.
Glenn T. Seaborg, Chairman of the United States Atomic
Energy Commission, put it straight, when at Georgetown
University in January of 1965 he said:

> Man may well have reached that point in his history, that
> stage of his development, where he has not only been made
> master of his fate, but where his technology and his morality
> have come face to face, where he can scarcely treat fact and
> value separately, and where he may see principles as diverse
> as the second law of thermodynamics and the Golden Rule
> being considered side by side in the making of decisions which
> determine his future.

Or to express it otherwise, Marshall McLuhan's "electric im-
plosion that compels commitment and participation" is inescapably part of his title for our time, "The Age of Anxiety."

City Plans
and City Planner

THREE

Our new, hard-earned image is that of a skilled and qualified professional working in concert with many others to provide an enlightened overview to community development. This skill is based upon a practical knowledge of the physical, political and socio-economic resources of the community.[1]

There are many professionals with whom interested churchmen must work in metropolis. Few will be encountered more often or in a wider range of common concerns than the city planner. It is of maximum importance to both, and to the city itself, that they understand each other. The basis of understanding is knowledge. As the churchman moves to implement his perspective in metropolis, he may well begin by knowing who the city planner is, and what he does.

---

[1]Robert L. Williams, Executive Director, American Institute of Planners, to the American Right of Way Association, Detroit, Michigan, May 25, 1964.

Planning as such is neither recent nor novel. The capacity to apply intelligent forethought to his activity is part of the nature of man. But planning as a distinct civic function is relatively new. In England it is known as town and country planning; here, as city and regional planning or, simply, urban planning. Planning is as intricate as the community it services. Aristotle suggests "security" and "happiness" as the purpose of cities. In metropolis the achievement of this double purpose requires an increasingly difficult convergence of programs, politics, people, and professionals.

The scope of planning is already frighteningly vast. It widens as man's option over his environment widens. "Nothing that is human is alien to city planning" is how one observer sees it, "and nothing in city planning can be alien to human nature."[2] The variety of "in-puts" into planning has always been great. It grows even greater: a) as cities and their problems become more complex, b) as the multitude of persons and programs which propose to deal with them becomes more numerous and more sophisticated, c) and as the urgency of interdisciplinary solutions becomes more inevitable.

There are many definitions of planning. In 1954, the United States Civil Service Commission described the task of the planner.

City Planners administer, advise on, supervise or perform professional work in the development of comprehensive plans, programs and regulations for the orderly physical growth

---

[2]Carol Aronovici, *Community Building* (Garden City, New York: Doubleday, 1956), p. 296.

and renewal of cities, towns, metropolitan areas and other population centers with the objective of promoting their economic, social and general welfare. Within statutory limits and in close cooperation with local authorities they collect, analyse, evaluate and present facts, trends and proposals, and develop integrated plans and recommendations for future growth and renewal. The work includes, among other items, consideration of population and income trends, construction costs, public finances, intergovernmental relationships and existing and future needs for land use, public utilities, community facilities, housing, circulation and transportation.

A political scientist calls planning "a process of understanding human needs and of influencing and shaping future public policy to serve those needs most effectively."[3] The English Schuster Report on "Qualification of Planners" adds:

The function is to create a well-balanced synthesis of what might otherwise be a mere collection of separate policies and claims, to combine them into one consistent policy for the use and development of land within the area in question; to devise the means of translating this policy in the physical conditions of that area into a plan that is practical, economic and aesthetically pleasing and to organize the carrying through to realization of the development for which the plan has made provision.[4]

Planning is research, analysis, diagnosis, and coherent prognosis.

The constitution of the American Institute of Planners

---

[3]Donald H. Webster, *Urban Planning and Municipal Public Policy* (Seattle, Washington: University of Washington Press, 1958), p. 4.

[4]"Qualification of Planners" (London: Ministry of Town and Country Planning, HMSO, 1950), p. 242.

calls planning "the unified development of communities as expressed through determination of the comprehensive arrangement of land uses and land occupancy and the regulation thereof."

To speak of the process of planning in singular terms is, of course, inaccurate. There are many different notions and countless variations in the semantics. Already in the earliest days it was clear to some that the process out of which plans emerged had to be different from that obtaining in any single discipline. Frederick Law Olmsted, for instance, told the first National Conference on City Planning in Washington, D. C., 22 May 1909:

> The ultimate purpose of city planning is not to provide facilities for certain kinds of transportation or to obtain certain architectural effects, but is to direct the physical development of the city by every means of control within the power of the municipality in such a manner that the ordinary citizen will be able to live and labor under conditions as favorable to health, happiness, and productive efficiency as his means will permit. Intelligent economy in the use of land and in construction and its maintenance is of the essence of the problem. It involves large questions of economics and social development and not merely those of engineering in the narrow sense or of architecture in the narrow sense.[5]

But if there is now agreement on the requirement for a broad approach to process, there has been no agreement on an exact definition of that process. For our purposes we break down the system by which plans are usually de-

[5]*Proceedings* published by the American Society of Planning Officials (September, 1967), pp. 65, 66.

veloped into simple stages. If the result is a kind of Guten-
berg Galaxy situation, at least this segregation of steps
permits a more reasonable inquiry into each of them.

There is, first of all, a goal stage. A careful assessment is
made of community values as nearly as they can be gathered
from official statements, surveys and personal analyses.
Their width and intensity of acceptance, their coherence
and their achievability are tested. They are related to each
other in long- and short-range categories. They are then ob-
jectified into purposes toward which the plan will be
directed. In the absence of explicit goals, direction is jerry-
built into the plan itself. Man acts for a purpose. Stated or
not, self-consistent or not, each plan moves some purposes
forward, retards others.

There is next a fact-finding and analysis stage. Sand-
wiched between two phases of the goal stage is data
collection. The community must know itself in actionable
dimensions. Resources and facilities, constraints and advantages must be tabulated and weighed together. Administrative, economic, and demographic situations must be
canvassed.

There is need at this point for a vertical element. The
community must know how it has come to where it is and
how, prospectively, it can go forward. It must understand
where and how it fits between neighborhood and nation.
Questions of prediction and extrapolation cannot, however,
be merely answered in terms of a gentle, arithmetic progression out of past speeds and trends. Everything in "the
electronic age" runs quicker. Everything is compressed into
faster motion. Programs for urban change are now unusually
numerous, unusually coherent, at least in concept. In short,

the prospects for drastic planned change in urban community are much more than a simple calculation forward in terms of observed past inadequacy and fragmentation.

There is need at this point, also, for a horizontal element. The community must know itself integratively and comparatively. It must be related to its neighbors, its region, its area. It can be inspired by what like communities have accomplished, warned by mistakes like communities have made. Especially as new programs develop, there is need for information as to how these programs have succeeded elsewhere.

There is, finally, need for an effective storage system for assembled information. This storage must involve easy retrievability. It must permit quick comparability, and it should invite action rather than delay it. Once the facts are in, the planner returns to his goal stage again. Goals must be re-examined in the light of the gathered data. Plan purposes must be balanced between recognition of constraints and resources and a clear vision as to what past experience, new programs, sometimes a maturing civic conscience suggest this community can become.

The next stage involves a proposition of alternative plans. Having assembled the data and rationalized the desires, the planner steps back, takes a long constructive look at the situation, picks up his color cans and his slide rule, flexes his professional imagination, and begins to sketch. He creates a series of planlets. These are broad-brushed, outline-type proposals. The number and refinement of them will depend on the nature and complexity of the circumstances and the time and planning resources available to him. Here the planner compares alternate methods for reaching a hierarchy of goals. Each planlet is assessed as it moves the community closer toward this goal, farther from that goal. What happens is a choice pattern which will run something like this:

	PLANLET A	PLANLET B	PLANLET C	PLANLET D
GOAL A				
GOAL B				
GOAL C				
GOAL D				
TOTAL				

In each box, the plusses and the minuses are quantified into a percentage of achievement. Variations in planlet components can be made which will later alter the totals in each box. Once he has completed this disjunction, grounded it and initially costed it, the planner feeds it into the political process. Sometimes this is quick and clean. Often it is long and complicated. Philadelphia's Edmund Bacon suggests that the contrivance of a satisfactory mutual decision as among alternatives will frequently require massive patience on the part of the planner. Coming into the council with his original preferred alternative, he meets questions and rejection. He must then, Bacon feels, re-group and return to the council again and again, amending there, adding here, until he has met the mind of political leadership and a firm beginning consensus has been achieved.

With this indication of preferred direction, the planner revises, details, and comes up with a final product—the plan.

Once again a decision is required. Once again an informed leadership yes is essential.

There are two further aspects to the planning process. Each must be adverted to throughout. Their importance increases at various places in the process. These two aspects are citizen participation and plan effectuation.

The involvement of the electorate is of major and growing significance in planning. Federal programs and common sense alike demand it. For the planner an involved citizenry must be a continuous pre-occupation at many points in the process and at several levels. He must, for instance, sell himself, his utility, his concern for "human scale" as well as his product. He must activate citizen support from the grass as well as the brass roots, city-wide as well as neighborhood, money men and developers as well as political leaders. His reports, for all their inevitable complexity, must speak also in simple, understandable and exciting language to the man in the urban street. All this will require much patience, enthusiasm, and optimism on his part, plus a great willingness to listen. Perhaps as much as is the clergyman, the planner is here commanded to the twenty-four-hour smile. It is too soon to say just how an increased emphasis in Federal programs on a participant poor will shake down in terms of effective participation. If not from the mass of citizens themselves, however, the planner can clearly anticipate a closer attention from those who claim to speak for a formerly inarticulate citizenry. His task, is, indeed, now complicated by the struggle for power among would-be citizen leaders whose title to representative recognition cannot be tested by customary political criteria.

Concern for effectuation, too, must be part of the entire

planning process. The planner who worries about implementing his plan only when it is complete cannot succeed. All the way along as many as possible of those who should be guided by it and whose cooperation will make or break it have to be involved as partners. If they remain jealously apart, competitive outsiders, the plan cannot succeed.

Activation of any plan, in fact, depends on three effective acceptances. It must be accepted by the citizens who elect and decide generally on the specific expenditures and timing of public action. It must be accepted by political leadership. It must be accepted with detailed understanding by operating civic departments. When the council stamps it approved, when it is aired in the news media, when it arrives at the desks of municipal department heads, it must be our plan rather than the planner's plan. Effectuation must include also check points and review provisions. The community will have to be reminded of the stage of completion at which the decided plan stands, of the obstacles it faces, of such amendments as it may require. Operating agencies must be checked and prodded to move it along.

The planning process, thus, is a matter of comprehending, relating, informing, budgeting, scheduling, gearing, and activating the little as well as the big decisions. It involves inevitably elements of science and art, poetry and prose.

As science it must be conversant with what the latest findings of the design and the behavioral sciences say to urban community. As science, planning is cybernetics, computers, standards, models. It is in this dimension that it reckons with the tough job of being viable, of comparable quantifications, of not leading man too far out beyond what he will or can accept.

As art, planning must be concerned with vision, aesthetics, space and spirit.

As poetry it must be rhymed through with lift and love, a thing of compassion as well as a thing of competence.

As prose it must be specific and clear enough so that what was wise in the general, will not be frustrated in the daily particular.

As it has developed over the years in the United States, planning relies on many tools and a few relatively simple base ideas. Its principal source is the police power. Back in 1789, police power was a plain prerogative of government to do all that was necessary to preserve the safety, health, and welfare of its citizens. It remains this, but its elasticity as quality rather than quantity now stretches much farther. Charles Abrams put it well:

> In the eighteenth century, the elder Pitt, Earl of Chatham, could declaim, "the poorest man in his cottage could defy the King—the storms may enter; the rain may enter—but the King of England cannot enter; all his forces dare not cross the threshold of the ruined tenement." But in the twentieth century, the king (or his counterpart, the state) may enter for the very purpose of keeping the wind and rain from entering. The "ruined tenement" has become a matter of state concern.[6]

In Euclid Village v. Ambler (1927) and in Berman v. Parker (1954) the United States Supreme Court declared zoning and urban renewal to be a legitimate part of the police power.

---

[6]*United Nations Housing and Town and Country Planning Bulletin #7, Urban Land Problems and* Policies (New York: United Nations, 1953), p. 1.

At the practical level, the central planning tool is the General Plan or, in renewal, its cousins the Community Renewal Plan and the Model Cities Plan. The General Plan is a series of maps and words in a pattern of fact and proposal covering an entire community. It has no binding legal effect in itself. It is implemented by statutes and departmental actions. It sets down for public agencies and concerned citizens alike, a statement of what the community is and a prospect of how it proposes to go forward. More particularly, the planner's tools include subdivision control ordinances, zoning, eminent domain, the official map, some involvement with municipal budgeting, a share in public land decisions, and various spot studies and proposals.

If there are any quick conclusions which sum up the state of city planning in the United States today, they are these:

1. increasingly as the community is goaded into new social conscience, planning must reflect this conscience;

2. more and more fine-grained data and research from more and more sources are available to the planner;

3. the urgency of planning regionally, as clusters of community rather than as single entities, becomes daily more obvious;

4. government urban programs proliferate with new requirements to comprehensiveness;

5. the dilemma of political effectiveness and yet sensitivity to the voices of the alienated, the disaffected, the apathetic poor remains. No early solution to it is in sight.

6. More and more professionals converge on what, for want of a better term, can be called applied urbanism or "urbanology."

The practice of planning, then, is centrally if controversially significant in metropolis. What of its practitioners?

The American Institute of Planners (AIP) in October, 1967, gave this "portrait of a typical community planner":

> He is under forty years of age, has entered the field since 1955 and earns between $7,500 and $12,000 annually. . . . Eighty one per cent of all AIP members want to take additional college courses, although over forty per cent already hold Master's degrees in planning and over ten per cent have Master's in other fields.

AIP itself has grown from twenty-four members in 1917 to about 5,000 today. The concerned churchmen will be working not so much with theories as with theoreticians and practicers.

What does the variable of personality, the pride and the prejudice, the finiteness add to the profession of planning— or subtract from it? Who is the city planner?

Inevitably, planners mirror the quandaries of their subject matter and their profession. They reflect the confidence and the frustration of urban possibilities. They image the self-uncertainty of an essentially interdisciplinary discipline.

Here is part of the chorus of contending advice in which the planner today works.

He is charged with negligence by critics like Jane Jacobs. She speaks of "the pseudoscience of city planning [based on] . . . the specious comfort of wishes, familiar superstitions, over-simplifications and symbols."[7]

He is taunted with having very little real power. Alvin Altshuler, in his unhappy profile of planning in the Twin Cities, is frank: "The political failures of general planning

---

[7]Jane Jacobs, *Death and Life of Great American Cities* (New York: Random House, 1961), p. 13.

have been notorious at all levels of American government."[8]

Land Lawyer Babcock speaks of the "general neurotic state of the planning profession"[9] and the "malaise of the planner"[10] He believes that the planner's role in society is unclear both to him and to those with whom he must deal.[11]

He is pushed toward politics. Governor Richard J. Hughes of New Jersey rejoiced at the American Society of Planning Officials meeting in Atlantic City in 1962: "Planners and politicians are bound together in a common cause."[12] He is urged often in his own publications to seek a service role in the political process. Robert C. Hoover calls him a suffering servant rather than a philosopher king. Norman Beckman notes "the similarity of the roles of the politician and the planner . . . the conflict thereby engendered; the vulnerability of the planner if he challenges the elected official for community leadership; the unique capability of the planner to serve the chief executive . . . [Planners must recognize], one, the dominant role of the politician in our governmental system; and two, the inevitable involvement of planners and other administrative generalists in the political process."[13] There has been much expert persuasion to the same effect.[14]

---

[8]Alan A. Altshuler, *The City Planning Process* (Ithaca, New York: Cornell University Press, 1965), p. 6.

[9]Richard F. Babcock, *The Zoning Game* (Madison, Wisconsin: University of Wisconsin Press, 1966), p. 62.

[10]*Ibid.*, p. 86.

[11]*Ibid.*, p. 86.

[12]*Planning 1962*, American Society of Planning Officials, p. 1.

[13]*AIP Journal* (November 1964), pp. 322, 323.

[14]See as example, addresses of the then Boston Redevelopment Administrator Edward J. Logue and then Associate Professor of Political Science at the Massachusetts Institute of Technology, Robert C. Wood, to the American Society of Planning Officials, as recorded in *Planning 1962*, pp. 5-14.

On the other hand, he is challenged to stand free of the Establishment, his ears and heart open as well to the cry of the unofficial poor as to City Hall. Paul Davidoff calls him to "advocacy and pluralism,"[15] suggesting that a mere mainstream political situation in fact stunts his integrity and unconscionably reduces his professional options. Grady Clay tells him:

> An outsider gets the impression that the planners may be running away, or at least moving away, from one of their traditional roles as a public defender and moving more deeply into the power structure of government. . . . It would be a sad day indeed if planners got taken over by government and if challenge and angry debate were left to the nongovernmenters—the League of Women Voters, the lobbyists, and the other people outside.[16]

Finally, the counsel planners receive from their elders is often disturbing:

> My experience in life as a social scientist and a social reformer has taken me far away from the simple trust in an easy and rapid advance through planning toward Eutopia, which was my spiritual heritage. I stick to the ideals from enlightenment as firmly as ever. But I am less hopeful about their early realization or even about the feasibility of an approach to it . . . I have been a planner all my life and will remain so. But I have increasingly been impressed by the staggering obstacles to overcome.[17]

---

[15]*AIP Journal* (November, 1965), pp. 331-337.
[16]*AIP Convention Proceedings*, 1965, p. 79.
[17]Gunnar Myrdal, Institute for International Economic Studies, University of Stockholm, in his address to the American Institute of Planners Convention, Washington, D.C., October 3, 1967.

Not all of this turmoil as to his role in the metropolitan game is an outside intrusion on him. A good deal of it descends to him from his history and his ancestry in the United States. In the early 1900's planning was mostly the hired hand of an independent commission, many times not even of public selection. Plans for Chicago and San Francisco, for instance, were funded by mercantile groups outside the political structure. Many of the earliest plans were spot documents concerned with new civic centers waterfront beautification, business districts. The plan for Chicago contains only a few sentences on slums. The idea was that planning should stand beyond politics, that it should be done by local Medici who by education, status, and perspective could think wise and long thoughts and who would not be subject either to bribery or to ballot boxes. These Medici would, the argument ran, relieve mayor and council of the tasks of long-range projection and would provide an objective, blue-ribbon base for community improvement. The prestige of the citizen planners would, further, encourage acceptance of their proposals by a grateful citizenry.

This initial direction proved inadequate for many reasons. The need for planning widened to include far more than spot suggestions for new trees and new civic centers. It became increasingly impossible to handle this need with volunteers who were, after all, only human and who were, even more importantly, removed from the control of those they proposed to plan for. As the potential bite of the planner in terms of specific municipal policies became evident, it became quickly evident also that executives, councils, and operating agencies responsible to the electorate could not be expected to recognize the overlordship of a committee installed in high non-elective, and unaccountable power.

Against this backdrop, two alternatives have suggested themselves. Somehow, both agree, the planner must be inserted into the political process. The first alternative in point of time was to associate the planner with the municipal executive. Here he functions at the mayor's right hand as part of the administration family. Ideally he correlates rather than competes with other municipal agencies. The second alternative proposes that the planner be structured close to the municipal legislature. The city council, in fact, reaches the daily decisions which make or break any plan. Kent sees the planner as working tandem to the council, advising it, involving it at all stages of plan preparation, assisting it to spell out for the operating agencies what action is required of them in terms of the plan.[18] Today, the picture is complicated by the resurgence of the original notion that planning must have continuous in-puts from people and power outside politics. Only this time that in-put is desired not so much from local Medici as from the participant poor, the "urban disadvantaged." The closer he sits, the more habitual his connection with and in the various levels of the Establishment, the more difficult it will be, the argument from advocacy continues, for him to accommodate interests which dissent from the municipal decision. The force of such an argument is multiplied if and as community action to relieve mass urban poverty is envisioned as requiring revolutionary changes in political procedures. In any case, the planner stands in metropolis today in a complexity of inherited and existential debate.

---

[18]T. J. Kent, *The General Plan* (San Francisco: Chandler Publishing Company, 1964).

To speak of the city planner singular, of course, is a mistake. He is legion. Planners range all the way from citizens who zone after supper on suburban planning boards to agency heads in city hall, urban renewers, and assessors. Richard F. Babcock in *The Zoning Game* and Roger Starr in *The Living End* are among those who explore in detail the role of citizen deciders in planning. The net conclusions are generally at best doubtful as to the future. The highway engineer plans; poverty warriors plan; conservationists plan. I concentrate here rather on the trained, degreed city planner. I do not overlook his un-degreed or otherwise degreed facsimile. Like Dennis O'Harrow of ASPO, I agree that "some of the best planners are planners, but likewise some of the best planners are not planners."[19] Simply, if planning is to be judged, it ought to be judged in terms of men who do it principally, out of a specific academic preparation, as their main task.

Fifteen years ago, John T. Howard, then president of the Institute, wrote an important editorial in the *Journal of the American Institute of Planners*. Its title was "Planning Is a Profession." In the article he listed these as some of the aspects of planning which qualified it for professional status:

    i. it is distinctly "tinged with public interest";

    ii. it involves a confidential relationship between the planner and his client, and this relationship requires that the personal interest of the planner be subservient to the interest of the client;

    iii. it is "predominantly intellectual . . . involving the consistent exercise of discretion and judgment";

---

[19]*Planning 1962*, p. 22.

iv. it requires "knowledge of an advanced type acquired by a prolonged course of specialized intellectual instruction."[20]

Since then, the debate continues as to the professionalism of planning. One thing is sure. It cannot be static because the field itself and the convergence of other professionals on it is far from static. The debate continues. It permeates each of the planner's own conventions. It is always high on the unwritten agenda of his neighbor professionals. One of its most significant expressions occurred recently in the State of New Jersey. Planners are neither registered nor licensed. In 1962, however, the State of New Jersey did pass a Professional Planners Act. This Act was the culmination of much political and topical interaction. It proposed to license planners to practice in New Jersey. All engineers, architects, and land surveyors licensed in their own professions in New Jersey were to be granted a planning license on application. Others could receive a license only on application and the successful completion of an examination. This included holders of AIP-recognized planning degrees. Supported by the American Institute of Architects and the American Society of Civil Engineers, this provision of the Act was opposed by the American Institute of Planners. On the one side it was argued that recognized competence in engineering and architecture should be sufficient to qualify a man, without further scrutiny, as a planner. Clearly this suggested that planning was not distinctly professional. It was argued by the American Institute of Planners that the Act discriminated against trained planners by requiring them to do more than appli-

---

[20]*AIP Journal* (Spring, 1954), p. 58.

cants who were not academically qualified to plan and that it overlooked the planner's professional status. Speaking through Judge Kingfield, the lower New Jersey Court found for the American Institute of Planners:

> The fact that historically planning evolved from architecture and engineering is of little or no consequence. This may be an unfortunate fact, but it is now recognized that the profession of planning is a separate and distinct profession. The evidence does not bear out the fact that an engineer, architect, or land surveyor by the education he has received and simply with the training in his respective field possesses the qualifications of a professional planner . . . by the law . . . professional planning is a separate profession.[21]

Appealed to the New Jersey Supreme Court, the decision was reversed. Much of the reversal pivots rather on the need for planners in New Jersey and on the question of separability of the provisions of the 1962 Act than on the validity of the planner's claim to a distinct professionalism. The issue of public safety is also considered. Obliquely, however, the matter of profession does arise. The decision says simply: "Achievement of licensure in one of the three named professions demonstrates sufficient minimal competence to engage in planning."[22]

The debate goes on. In most instances, planners themselves hold for professionalism. They cite the usual criteria of a profession: expert training in a definable skill, expert literature,

---

[21]New Jersey Chapter, American Institute of Planners v. State Board of Professional Planning, February 26, 1966.
[22]New Jersey Chapter, American Institute of Planners v. State Board of Professional Planning, February 20, 1967.

a formal expert association, public service dedication. They claim that more than three dozen planning schools provide the first, that the American Institute of Planners, now past its fiftieth anniversary, provides the second and third, and that the very nature of planning provides the fourth. The churchman approaching the planner can decide for himself whether these claims are correct. At least he will need to recognize that, conceding a frequent fraying around the edges, planners consider themselves professionals. The mere charge that they are in constant debt to and collaboration with a wide variety of other professionals is not in itself sufficient to deny the validity of their self-statement. Certainly any reasonable estimate of the quality of the discipline must be based first on how planners themselves view their trade rather than on what not always unselfish neighbors say about it.

Whatever his exact position in the company of urban professionals, there are three background aspects of the city planner which the churchman will need to notice as he estimates him. Who become city planners? How are they trained? What is their personal situation as a group in metropolis?

The in-put into planning is broad. What it is which moves a young man (or a young woman) in later undergraduate years toward planning as a vocation has never been fully determined. One thing is certain—there is no monolithic entry pattern. In most cases, even, there is no decision toward planning until well along in undergraduate years. There have been some surveys of motivation to planning. There are certainly a number of possibilities. These include the following:

1. A feeling on the part of the undergraduate that he has

gone about as far as he can in his prospective field of study, but wants to go farther. This becomes a felt need to push back the walls which limit him in his own first choice of vocation.

2. A great desire to combine a profitable career with public service. It remains debatable how recognition of a notably undersupplied demand balances against the possibility of wielding a benevolent public power as a motivating factor.

3. A growing awareness that inter-disciplinariness, far from being a luxury for doctoral candidates, has become a part of the warp and woof of metropolis and that in planning, interdisciplinariness is proudly acknowledged and continuously necessary.

At the very core is a kind of mystical humanitarianism which attracts the idealist as well as a kind of tangible sense of comprehension and control which attracts the realist. This combined physical and social pull to planning, this variety of motivation, is reflected in the student body at all planning schools. At Catholic University, of our seventy-three graduate planning students in September, 1967, twenty-four were architects, nineteen engineers, five economists, five landscape architects. Our first graduate came out of sociology; our second, out of geography; our third, from economics; our fourth, from architecture. There has been some shifting of student backgrounds over the years, but the picture remains fairly constant. In 1951-1952, 38% of planning students in the United States held degrees in architecture, 11% in engineering.[23] In 1965, 38% of those who graduated from

---

[23]Harvey Perloff, *Education for City Planning* (Baltimore, Maryland: Johns Hopkins University Press, 1957).

American graduate schools of planning started with undergraduate backgrounds in architecture and engineering. In 1966 the figure rose to 41%.[24] In 1958-1959 the composition of the American Institute of Planners was

24% architecture background,
20% landscape architecture background,
13% engineering background (mainly civil),
 7% sociology background,
 6% economics background,
 5% political science background,
20% miscellaneous background.[25]

This variety complicates and enhances the entire matter of planning education. There is no reasonable prospect of its diminution. Quite the contrary, every likelihood is for even more variation in in-put as areas of planning preoccupation widen and the range of possible situations into which the planning graduate may emerge proliferates.

Planning education began formally in the United States with courses at the University of Illinois in the 1910's and at Harvard in the 1920's. Harvard authorized what is considered the first full planning degree in 1929, MIT shortly thereafter. At the outbreak of World War II there were four American schools of planning: Harvard, MIT, Cornell, and Columbia. Today there are more than three dozen schools. Students enrollments at these schools are:

---

[24]American Society of Planning Officials' *1966 Survey of Planning Schools.*

[25]Altshuler, p. 393. These figures represent questionnaire replies correlated in an unpublished University of North Carolina planning master's thesis by Lucien F. Faust.

	1963-1964	1965-1966
a. Actual Enrollment toward Planning Bachelor's Degree	150	302
Actual Planning Bachelor's Degrees Awarded	61	73
b. Actual Enrollment toward Planning Master's Degree	688	956
Actual Enrollment Master's Degrees Awarded	316	347
Actual Planning Schools Reporting	32	37
c. Actual Enrollment toward Ph. D. in Planning	68	92
Actual Ph. D.'s in Planning Awarded	10	10[26]

Several conclusions emerge. Expansion in numbers is the rule at all levels. The Master's degree remains by far the majority situation. Significant increases, however, occur at both the Bachelor's and Doctor's degree levels. It is too soon for authoritative estimates on what this reawakening of interest in the Bachelor's degree and in more numerous Ph. D's will do for the profession in time. Nor is a realistic judgment possible as yet on certain tentative programs directed toward the training of planning technicians in a junior college context.

The Master's program as it has developed since World War II has been fairly constant. Students enter from a very wide range of backgrounds. Inevitably their preparations are also diverse. Undergraduate inadequacies are variously

[26]ASPO 1966 *Survey of Planning Schools.* In its *May 1968 Newsletter,* ASPO adds the following at page 43:

In the 10 school years ending June 1967, U. S. planning schools had granted 3,161 degrees: PhD—60; MA—2,422; and BA—679. In 1967-1968 the 46 U.S. schools covered in the survey anticipated that 814 degrees would be awarded, more than one-fourth of the total for the preceding 10 years. The estimate was for 24 PhD's, 650 MA's, and 140 BA's.

handled. Some planning schools include threshold competence courses in their first-year curriculum. There are apt
to be courses in urban sociology, on the one hand, for architects and engineers, and in introduction to design, on the
other hand, for behavioral scientists. These courses are tail-
ored to bring the new student up to a beginning level of
competence in areas with which he is not familiar. Other
schools require entrance examinations in subject matter for
which the student's training is not sufficient. Failure to pass
these examinations means that the student must supplement
his regular planning curriculum with additional courses in
the area of failure.

Generally, the Master's program envisions a two-year
period of study with thesis, though there are tendencies to
lengthen this time to two and one-half or three years. Summer internship in a planning office is required. The first year
is usually a syndrome of required courses. The second year
is mostly guided electives. The required component of planning education includes, as might be anticipated, transportation, history and theories of cities, planning laws, housing
and renewal, metropolitan organization, the politics and
economics of planning. Electives can range over a great area
of choice, depending on the student's need and option. At the
Catholic University of America we specify forty-two hours
for all candidates for the Master's in City and Regional Planning degree. Thirteen of these hours are elective, the other
twenty-nine are required. These twenty-nine break down
as follows:

CRP #549 Transportation for Planners   3 Credits
CRP #551 Planning Principles I   3   "

CRP #552 Planning Principles II 3 Credits
CRP #554 Planning the Region 3 "
CRP #555 Quantitative Planning 2 "
CRP #556 Planning Methods 3 "
CRP #557 Federal Urban Programs 2 "
CRP #558 Housing 2 "
CRP #560 Planning Problems I (City) 3 "
CRP #567 Planning Problems II (Region) 3 "
CRP #568 Urban Economics 2 "

Most planning courses are lecture and seminar. There is a heavy admixture of application assignments either alone or in groups. Problem courses are the real workhorse of planning education. They are set up as microcosms of an actual community planning experience. In them the planning student is trained in the application-by-doing of his class knowledge to actual chunks of urban land and, increasingly, to the human perplexities of actual neighborhoods and regions. Teams of students, carefully associated from different backgrounds, are grouped and directed toward a located problem. The student must research that situation, analyze it, conclude, and then adjust his conclusions with those of his teammates into a viable series of maps, proposals, models, and ideas. Each team must defend itself in competition with other teams before a "jury" of professionals and relevant citizens.

This process, obviously, affords the student a number of learning experiences. He is required to close-end his theories in a context of constraints and with his eye on an invincible clock. He is required to present and defend his ideas much as he will be forced to do later in his agency and before his public constituency. He is habituated to working with others from different disciplinary perspectives in a coordinated approach to a common problem.

There are, admittedly, difficulties with the problems method, but in general it works. Or at least it habituates the student to recognize severe time constraints and the difficulty of reaching an effective consensus. It also functions to defeat in the sweat of common challenge stereotypes which have tended to poison the attitude of one professional to others.

I have jokingly referred to planning education as a combination of Dale Carnegie courses and the Berlitz School. I mean it. Public relations expertise as well as the ability to understand many professional languages are key requirements in planning. The planner must understand widely and communicate persuasively. Put another way, the planner must throughout his student years be conscious of the fact that inevitably he must work as a professional in a shifting range of situations on the sides and along the diagonals of at least this rectangle of concern:

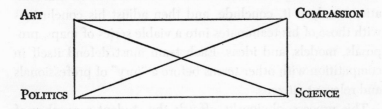

His whole education is calculated to help him talk to those he meets en route through his rectangle, then to express and sell the coherent message he derives from his conversation.

Planning education has for its principal objective the development of a professional who is aware of his limitations, but schooled in the grace of coherence, and who can propose to man upon a given piece of earth, a reasonably viable community vision. It is, of course, impossible for any single professional to comprehend totally all the factors which influence any urban situation. It is possible, however, to approach closer to such comprehension. What is important here is not the conclusion so much as the process itself. The planner's best judgment, as it emerges from his formal education, will be flawed with uncertainty and imperfection, just as urban man himself is uncertain and imperfect. What really matters is that the planner will have trained himself to an increasing regard for the theory and practice of all the other urban arts and sciences. He will be habitually associational. The point has seldom been better made than by Robert C. Hoover:

> The planner must not try to outdo the specialists at their own games but help them to transcend their technical narrowness so that they too become planners by relating their work to broader concern. Far from fearing the jurisdictional intrusions of the established disciplines, the planner welcomes them gladly to dialogue.[27]

For all his breadth, however, the planner must leave the planning school a closed-end disciplinarian. Whatever the sprawling of his ideas about people in urban space, he must be operable. This whole process is not so simple as it seems. To retire too soon from the pursuit of perfection can be

---

[27] *AIP Journal* (November, 1961), p. 294.

a fault. Planners may indeed be at times over-timid about the potential for radical change in the forces which shape metropolis. Still, the fact remains. Unless the planner can catalyze a neighborhood, influence land decisions in a real city with a real mayor and council, help shape an actual region, talk about neighborness, cityness, regionness is idle gymnastry. The planning student continues to find his home more naturally with the closed-end design disciplines. I do not mean to suggest that he can ever retire into the fortresses of architecture and engineering, banging shut some great portcullis after him. I do mean that in a universe in which all urban professions move toward each other, or at least toward a recognition that each has a practical contribution to make, the still customary placement of planning education in proximity to the design sciences continues to make sense. Planning in metropolis simply cannot wait until there are total answers to every social problem of urban man.

Mostly, the churchman will meet the planner practicing. This planner will have come to his post from one of many backgrounds, but, increasingly, from a formal graduate education similar to that just discussed. The operating planner, as the student planner, wrestles with several principal problems. The first is a problem of self-identity, of scope. What is planning after all? Is it big? Does it cover everything and everyone who proposes in any sense to develop parts of or all metropolitan areas? Is it small, circumscribed by land use specifically? Is it rather information assembly and systematic data organization by physically skilled technicians? The planner can take some comfort from the knowledge that his neighbor professionals operate in similar crises of self-identity. But the dilemma remains, with its psychological and professional unease. Practice as well as theory is involved.

There is a second problem, the curious question of polarization. The planner will be tempted to quick answers, to simple remedies. Particularly as those who are unschooled in the sophistications and the nuances of urban life but are desperately concerned with its observed inadequacies take power in our cities, the problem will grow. As the need for instant remedies increases, so will the pressure to simplification and immediate actions. Again an intelligent planning decision here is difficult. It has been written of urban renewal:

> Renewal requires the avoidance of false dichotomies to prevent the total polarization of conflicting values. It proceeds only as the participants are willing to compromise on specific points at issue while never compromising the integrity of the participants. It is productive only if new values, greater than those in conflict, are established.[28]

Melvin Webber testifies to the break-down of "black-white, yes-no, push-pull, either or dichotomies."[29] Yet, to galvanize minorities to action, to motivate the citizenry of cities, things sometimes must be shaken down into simple terms. In the resolution of this dilemma, the planner will require much patience and perception.

A third difficulty involves the location of the planner in the spectrum of urban influences. How does he fit in? What are his optimal working relationships with his neighbors?

---

[28]Leo Molinaro, then President of the West Philadelphia Corporation in *Colloquy*, published by the Christian Association at the University of Pennsylvania (April, 1967), p. 20.

[29]*AIP Journal* (November, 1965), pp. 289-296.

Perhaps one can never reach the vision of Patrick Geddes: "Scientist and artist . . . begin to understand and trust each other; a true cooperation begins. This is a new age; a new enthusiasm, a new enlightenment are already dawning."[30]

Important beginnings, however, have been made. In 1964 an Interprofessional Committee on Environmental Design (ICED) was established. It linked the American Institute of Architects, the American Society of Civil Engineers, the American Society of Landscape Architects, and the American Institute of Planners in permanent association. While there is no such formal inter-relationship on the "social" side,[31] contacts inevitably multiply. Indeed, planning conventions have long been noted for a massive array of speakers from both the behavioral and design sciences. It would be a mistake, of course, to suggest that all the associational problems have vanished, that we have become somehow a harmonious group of urban professionals all understanding and working together. Frictions and fictions survive. Stereotypes remain: stereotypes of architects as arty and expensive dreamers, of engineers as blind mechanics, of social workers as fuzzy-wuzzies ignorant of cost and physical-fiscal context, of planners as narrowly physical people with color

---

[30]Patrick Geddes, *Cities in Evolution* (London: Norgate and Williams, 1953), p. 158.

[31]A good deal of thought and some organizational tentatives, however, are being directed toward this problem. For instance, an American Institute of Urban and Regional Affairs has just been established at a charter meeting in May, 1968, in Atlanta, Georgia. Its announced purpose is:

to understand the urban influence upon the development and control of social, behavioral and environmental problems (and to promote) . . . the application of the knowledge and methods of the social sciences to urban and regional affairs.

It is still, of course, far too soon to predict the future of this Institute. The author is a member of its Research and Grants Committee.

cans and computers, but no heart! In addition, as community development becomes more and more profitable for the expert, and its dimensions become more and more complex, the pressures of competition, of misunderstanding, are amplified. "Urban affairs" is no longer an erudite luxury either for university or professional. It is a profitable and exciting challenge for student, administration, and faculty alike. The operating planner, like St. Sebastian stands pierced by many arrows in many parts of his anatomy and thrown from many hands. With one of the newest professions, he must live closely and productively not only with alienated or negatively powered citizens, but also with two of the oldest and most honorable professions on earth, architecture and engineering. More and more he is expected to solve problems which society itself has not solved. The matter he works with, too, becomes increasingly intricate. Berkeley's John W. Dyckman writes:

> The contemporary city planner faces not only the complexity of the modern metropolis, but also the exploding discretionary range of behavior made available by abundance. . . . Urbanization is a process which stands for a whole cluster of other processes, and for scores of social and economic variables.[32]

Fifty years ago Patrick Geddes wrote, "Our task is rendered more difficult by the immensity of the materials."[33] Even for the urban citizen, in the words of Leonard Reissman, "The city is without doubt the most complex environment devised

---

[32]*Environment for Man*, papers delivered at the American Institute of Planners convention in Portland, Oregon, August, 1966 (Bloomington, Indiana: the University of Indiana Press, 1967), pp. 28, 43.

[33]Geddes, p. 2.

by man and to understand it and his place in it, he must recognize the complexity of the relationship."[34]

Perhaps nowhere more than in the profession which works with metropolis as both physique and psyche, moneys and moods, is complexity a continuous presence. The situation is almost impossibly diverse, yet in it the planner must contrive so to simplify that coherent action can be staged, budgeted, accomplished, and continued. He knows how much sense he makes. He is sure that his stock in trade is of major importance to metropolis. But he is more and more frustrated by the pressures on him, more and more conscious of the ever-impossible challenge under which he moves toward comprehensiveness. The fact that so much planning has had so little success in the United States is not the really remarkable thing at all, but rather the fact that we have come as far with planning as we have. In so many ways, while he makes great common sense, the planner runs counter to his time. He preaches sublimation of the immediate and the self into the long-range and collective good. His purpose is commonwealth. He preaches to an age which revels in its anarchy, refuses to wait any longer for urban justice, apotheosizes the selfishness of individual and group, and generally scoffs at municipal prudence. It is hardly surprising, even were he himself perfect or his product ideal, that he encounters rejection.

One of the most difficult dilemmas which confronts the practicing planner is to determine where he should professionally stand along the line between humbleness and

---

[34]Leonard Reissman, *The Urban Process* (Glencoe, Illinois: Free Press, 1964), p. 121.

self-confidence. Robert C. Hoover, in a most perceptive article, calls him to service.[35] Ardee Ames, then Assistant to the President of Reston New City, Virginia, tells him that such service must be at best limited:

> ... perhaps you as planner find it hard to accept the underlying reality that the growth and shape and form and character of the cities is pretty much determined by the multitude of decision-makers and organizations who are putting up the money and, therefore, are going to call the tune—whether entitled to or not. I suspect that all the planner can really do is to provide the informational ammunition in terms of the program that he thinks best, and he can try to do whatever he can within the limits of his own energy, time limitations, and job security limitations to influence the decision-makers and the money spenders.[36]

Roger Starr warns:

> Having been told that he must be democratic, the planner assumes that democracy means that he cannot demand precedence for his plans over the wishes of any individual. It is fair to say, I think, that planners suffer from a moral inferiority complex in the presence of anti-planners. ... Until planners once again have confidence in the moral justification of their endeavors, their effort to plan effectively for their cities is doomed to nervousness, disappointment, and fatal compromise. I say to you that the belief in the wisdom and justification of joint action rests on solid grounds; I hope you will be able to stop looking over your shoulder at your philosophical critics. The greatest chances lie ahead of you.

---

[35] *AIP Journal* (November, 1961).
[36] *AIP Convention Proceedings*, 1965, p. 77.

He continues:

> Planners, therefore, stand in a uniquely favorable position to effectuate that compromise between the general and the specific on which sound government depends. I ask you, as planners, not to abandon your conviction that the will of The People stands on high moral ground, limited only by the individual rights of persons set forth in the basic law of the land. Until planners once again have confidence in the moral justification of their endeavors, their effort to plan effectively for their cities is doomed to nervousness, disappointment, and fatal compromise.[37]

This tug between savior and servant, self-assured voice of the public majority and hired hand to the loudest power factor in his community, is rendered even more confusing by the absence of total comprehensiveness and yet the urgency for action. The planner is aware of his own partial vision, of his own limited talents, of the sheer shortages of time. Yet he must intervene somehow here and now in this urban circle,* knowing that intervention at any point must impact at other points.

Seldom have the dimensions of the planner's dilemma been more sharply evident than at the 1967 convention of their professional organization. If we are to understand that dilemma, we ought to reflect at some length on this convention.

On the first of October, 1967, 3,000 planners convened at the Shoreham Hotel in Washington, D.C. The occasion was a six-day anniversary conference of the American Institute of Planners. The theme was "The Next Fifty

---

[37]*Planning 1966*, ASPO, pp. 133, 136.
*See next page.

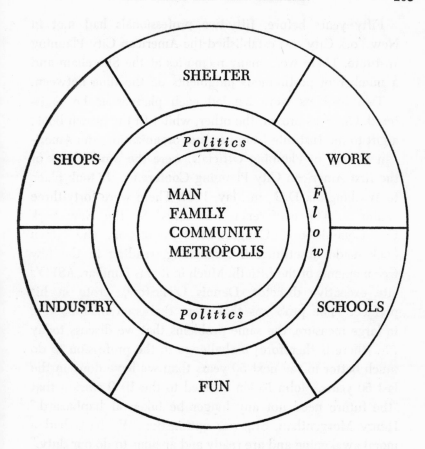

Years." Surrounded by gay vertical square banners which made a patchwork quilt image of "an environment for man" and titillated by McLuhan-like sense displays, the planners sat through one of the most intensive and extensive collections of erudite sermons ever preached in one place to so polyglot a congregation. Fittingly for men and women who propose, as viceroys for commonwealth, to remake metropolis, the conference began in the Regency Room! A new urban stamp was issued.

Fifty years before, fifty-two professionals had met in New York City and established the American City Planning Institute. There were many memories at the Shoreham and a number of posthumous judgments on the time between.

Two booklets were handed each planner as he registered. One was brown; the other, white. In the brown book, a gift to the Institute from its sister organization, the American Society of Planning Officials, were the proceedings of the first American City Planning Conference. It took place in Washington, D.C., in May, 1909. There were forty-three conferees. The conference was called by the New York City Committee on Congestion of Population. The brown book made unsettling, if fascinating, reading in the few free moments of the fiftieth. Much in it was familiar. ASPO's late executive director, Dennis O'Harrow, wrote in his preface: "The problems that were discussed in 1909 are, in large measure, the same problems that we discuss today . . . [there is therefore] a challenge to the profession to do much better in the next 50 years than we have done in the last 50 years." John Nolen boasted to the 1909 session that "the future need not any longer be taken at haphazard." Henry Morgenthau, Sr., was optimistic: "We have had a moral awakening and are ready and anxious to do our duty." Frederick Law Olmsted was less sanguine: "Here in America we seem to go on complacently perpetuating our old mistakes long after we have recognized them . . . [I am troubled by] this hopeless fatalism in our attitude toward the more fundamental factors of city growth."

No planner could read the brown book without discovering in it at once a great urgency and a great euphoria about the nation's urban future. No planner who read the brown book fifty years later could do so without a sense of bitter-sweet ambivalence. So much remained undone, and yet so many had tried valiantly in so many places with limited resources to reach the critical horizons of a planned commonwealth. And at least the planning idea had caught on. It had long since grown big enough to be at least seriously debated. At the Conference on May 22, 1909, Speaker of the House of Representatives Joseph G. Cannon had told the planners: "I bid you godspeed in this planning that you are working for, but for heaven's sake don't follow the example of some and try to relieve conditions that you don't understand." Brown book in hand, the planners at the Shoreham could be happy in the knowledge that they had widened their understanding and were resolutely grappling with problems from an ever-widening base of empathy. Inevitably, though, the flaming streets of the summer of 1967 reminded them they had not yet solved the radical human problem of cities.

The white book was done for AIP by veteran planner Russell Van Nest Black. It was a kind of biography of the professional institute and the planner over the past half century. In the white book, John Nolen's three criteria for judging planning were set down.

The first criterion was the number of professionals and the frequency of professional involvement. "Quantitatively," said the white book, "planning has made great headway. . . . Rare now is the town, city, or county even remotely concerned with urban matters that is not engaged in organized planning of one sort or another." The second criterion concerned the quality of the planning effort and production. The qualitative measure is more elusive! The judgment:

Accepted planning principles have become increasingly evident over the years in city building . . . It is in its influence upon the total urban environment that planning may seem to have failed. . . . In this respect planning is in something of the position of the boy plugging the hole in the dyke with his thumb.

The third criterion was a comparative rating of planning progress with that of other community-concerned disciplines. This criterion considered "advances in the art and science of planning as compared with the advances in other fields of human endeavor." Here the conclusion was frank: "It [planning] is in the dark ages when weighed against the advances in those sciences that have split the atom, cleared the way to open-heart surgery, enabled visual communication around the globe, and are in a fair way to landing men on the moon." But this state of art, the white book said, was only par for the course. In its failure to reach levels of breakthrough achieved in other hard science disciplines, planning was only mirroring like failure in most of the behavioral sciences: "Planning, along with governmental organization upon which it so much depends, lags behind the more exact sciences only as do all other of the arts and sciences having to do with man's relation to man." The white book concluded: "Planning, in its larger bearing upon community welfare, can advance only as the people advance in their concept of what the city ought to be and what their individual contribution to the making of that city can and must be."

However, the past is sliced, it was clear that the issue here was critical throughout the fiftieth. How does one measure the planner's success in society? As one urban professional, partial in his reach, however comprehensive he may be in his hope, can the planner rightly be faulted for the failure of society as a whole to underwrite bright new cities with sustained popular support? Or, as editor Perry Prentice put it to the fiftieth-anniversary gathering on October 5: "How come, year after year, despite all your planning, all your efforts and all your dreams, how come most of our big American cities seem to be getting so much worse instead of better?"

I remain personally convinced that the planner need not apologize for his inability to shake the whole fabric and conscience of society. Much of his so-called failure must be assessed to the orneriness, finiteness, and ignobility of collective man rather than to the admitted smallness and early imperfections of the profession. As a German planner wrote after his visit to the United States,

> In the course of my trip to the United States, the impression ripened that [there is a] crisis of society of which the planners, in spite of honest self-criticism, are not yet conscious. They are looking for the shortcomings in their own rank, while in fact they often seem to be the scapegoats of a society which cries out for planning yet repels it as incompatible with its traditions and the sacred principles of unlimited individual freedom and oppotunity.[38]

A second issue which was tossed early into the conference hopper was the issue of advocacy. This issue, quite simply, focused on whether planners should relate as professionals and as citizens more directly than has been the case till

---

[38]*April 1965 Newsletter*, ASPO.

now to organized groups operating outside the traditional politics of the community. In an area up for urban renewal, for example, should planners be hired or volunteer to work up plans for neighborhood associations which would then compete with officially prepared plans? The net result, it was argued, would be a better recognition of the rights of the poor and a survival-of-the-fittest plan in the end. Paul Davidoff, head of Hunter College's Planning Program, had written a moving article "Advocacy and Pluralism in Planning" in the *American Institute of Planners Journal*:

> The advocacy of alternative plans by interest groups outside government would stimulate city planning in a number of ways.
> First, it would serve as a means of better informing the public of the alternative choices open, alternatives strongly supported by their proponents. . . . A second way . . . would be in forcing the public agency to compete with other planning groups to win political support. . . . A third improvement . . . would be to force those who have been critical of 'establishment' plans to produce superior plans rather than only to carry out the very essential obligation of criticizing plans deemed improper.[39]

On Sunday, 1 October 1967, Davidoff addressed the Association of Collegiate Schools of Planning. He called for an activist involvement of the planning student in pre-advocacy. Students, he proposed, must get their hands dirty in actual street commitment, in community action programs, in the nitty-gritty details of neighborhood politics! The conference had not been in session but a very few hours when Davidoff

---

[39]*AIP Journal* (November, 1965), pp. 332, 333.

(and others) carried his message to an organization known as Planners for Equal Opportunity (PEO). PEO had existed before. Davidoff had for some time been one of its key people. In Washington at the fiftieth it made much noise. PEO sessions were scheduled simultaneous with the conference program; considerable attention was attracted from the news media. The proposition was frankly for a more activist planner, for openly grass-roots planning.

There were many reactions to the Davidoff-PEO approach. Some conferees applauded; some opposed; most distinguished. The debate which resulted was one of the most persistent items in the entire conference.

The argument started with a consensus that planners must be "sensitized" to politics. This sensitizing must include not only politics as practiced through an orderly ballot box, political parties and bureaucracy, but also politics as practiced by *ad hoc* activist groups in discontented urban neighborhoods. There was no doubt that as much as possible planners need to know how plain people feel as well as how the chain of command and the red tapes run at city hall and in Federal offices. All seemed to agree, finally, that the summer riots of 1967 as well as model-cities legislation and "civil rights" spoke imperatively to the planner.

Those who concurred with the Davidoff-PEO approach went further into advocacy and outright activism. Those who did not concur suggested that: a) planners are no more social workers or political scientists than they are architects or engineers; b) to expect them to be experts in community organization and the ways of poor power is as unreal as to expect them to be experts in computer hardware or ultimate Baumeisters; c) the emotionalism involved in total identification with a polarized street group can very easily become detrimental to a responsible professional planning judgment; d) while all astigmatism must be resisted, astigmatism can be as much a part-thing as a whole-thing; and e) it is as inimical to good planning, perhaps even more inimical, for planners to espouse the astigmatism of one aroused neighborhood or of one interest in cities as it is for them, without taking thought, to espouse the astigmatism of a city hall presumably speaking for the power structures.

The debate was, of course, not resolved. It was clear that the planners at the Shoreham were being torn between several value poles — first, the value of succeeding with their plans; second, the value of a professional judgment which could not be finally decided by majority vote; third, the ethics of seeking to represent the greatest possible number of citizens and to respond to the greatest dimension of human hurt and need; fourth, the imperative lesson of flaming streets. Even after fifty years of "working through channels," no really massive social changes have been worked by planning in metropolis. And yet there is a clear need in any profession for what I call professional cool (*not* cold). I mean by this that a professional requires the moment of withdrawal and the ability to stand apart for purposes of a reasoned analysis of the situation in which he must be professional as well as the moment of return and contact, if he is effectively and honestly to estimate that situation and build forward from his estimate. This is especially so when the professional's commodity is community. What Roger Starr said about "people" and "the people" in his address to the ASPO in Philadelphia in 1966 is also clearly relevant. The decision as to who and how the planner's constituency is cannot be a function only of angry involvement in specific streets with loud local leaders.

A third issue at the conference appeared on Sunday morning at the meeting of the Collegiate Schools of Planning and ran throughout. It involves what C. David Loeks, immediate past president of the Institute, calls "the diversity-circumscription debate."[40] The issue has two aspects. One is the professional's view of himself. The other is the scope and definition of the profession itself. Is the planner a nine-to-five bureaucrat doing one very largely fiscal-physical job in an administration team? Is his task quite simply to contribute what he can out of a limited specialty and a gloss of generalism, not bothering much with after-hours advocacy or the pursuit of more and more knowledge about cities? Should planning as a profession opt for a closely circumscribed area of competence and action? Should the professional and the profession, on the other hand, opt rather for an increasingly broad understanding of man in metropolis, seek to maximize the variables which enter planning decisions rather than restrict them to an actionable brevity?

As has already been indicated, this issue was not new at the conference. It has been a moot point for years. There were many nuances to it. For instance, Robert C. Hoover in a now classic article had proclaimed:

> Planners are . . . challenged to . . . hard work in understanding sympathy with the family of specialists and professionals concerned with urban growth . . . A genuine planner

---

[40]*AIP Convention Proceedings*, 1965, p. 13.

. . . far from fearing jurisdictional intrusions by the established disciplines, welcomes them. For only in this way does the planning dialogue become a full multilogue. Thus emerges this distinguishing and unique difference between planning and other related professions. While other professions draw boundaries which keep other people out, planning draws an ever widening circle to bring others in.[41]

In a way perhaps, planners were reaching back to the comprehensive ideas of John Henry Cardinal Newman who had written in his *Idea of a University*:

That only is true enlargement of mind which is the power of viewing many things at once as one whole, of referring them severally to their true place in the universal system, of understanding their respective values, and determining their mutual dependence.[42]

What he wrote further in this area of concern is clearly relevant to the dilemma in which American planning finds itself at mid-adolescence:

[We must beware of] the error of distracting and enfeebling the mind by an unmeaning profusion of subjects; of implying that a smattering in a dozen branches of study was not shallowness, which it really is, but enlargement; of considering an acquaintance with the learned names of things and persons and the possession of clever duodecimos and attendance on eloquent lectures, and memberships with scientific institutions, and the sight of experiments of a platform and the specimens of a museum, that all this was not dissipation of the mind but progress.

---

[41]*AIP Journal* (November, 1961).
[42]John Henry Cardinal Newman, *The Idea of a University* (London: Longmans, Green, and Company, 1859), Discourse VI.

Every great metropolis, Newman believed, is a university. MIT's Kevin Lynch, in his address at the fiftieth, kept referring to the "educative" city. He pleaded for a greater empathy on the part of the planner, not only with mass statistics in cybernetic systems, but also with the emotions and the eyes and ears of the city. There is, however, so very much to be watchful over. And Marshall McLuhan has well noted that the price of eternal vigilance is indifference. As the so-called second Malthusian law has it, information multiplies faster than the ability of man to absorb it, much less interrelate its categories. It seems evident, in any case, that the debate over "circumscription" and "diversity" will go on and that it will come to rest only now and then along a continuum from an impossible omniscience to a culpable ignorance of meaningful variables. Perhaps the best approach is simply to withdraw the planner more and more within his design and managerial competences. Perhaps he need only specialize in three areas, leaving the rest to his converging neighbor professionals: first, in knowing how to combine the discoveries of those neighbors; second, in knowing how to express that combination in viable proposals; third, in knowing how to move such proposals through politics and market into at least partial accomplishment. Perhaps, indeed, he must relate to the theoreticians of society, the activists and the poverty warriors as consumer rather than as producer, much as he has in the past related in their fields of expertise to the architect and the engineer. Perhaps he must be an intensely interested observer, involved, but fundamentally technical rather than substantive in the tensions of human change in metropolis.

One of the most noticeable aspects of the fiftieth was a marked increase in the presence of men of religion among

the planners.[43] In previous conferences some clergy had been
in evidence. There was sometimes a local blessing, a
sprinkling of native clerics. But here in the Shoreham identifiable clergy were numerous. There were dozens of them in
the cloth. There were many others who wore street clothes
and so did not stand out. Proceedings opened with an invocation. The new urban stamp was launched with a first
blessing by a clergyman from the Twin Cities, who was also
an alderman, and by a priest-planner. Even if one discounts
a large contingent of National Council of Churches recruits,
some of whom presumably came out of loyalty, this kind of
clerical presence demands analysis. Once again, Roman
Catholic participation was shockingly minimal. I talked with
many of the clergy. No pattern is, of course, possible, but I
believe these conclusions are justified:

1. At least some important people in the churches in the
United States, and a growing number of locally involved
churchmen, are becoming aware of the need for a much
greater sophistication in religion's reach toward new
metropolitan relevance.

2. It is becoming clearer to most churchmen that, in
addition to crying protest before injustice, they must study
and understand the very complex problems of urban change
if they are responsibly to help solve them.

3. A new dialogue between religion and planning seems
now possible and, from both standpoints, desirable.

4. The time seems to be here when churches and plan-

43William H. Claire, in *AIP Journal* (Fall, 1964), p. 177.

ners need to ponder the best forms for their future interaction at both the national and the local levels.

5. The churches' plant-and-program situations are being seriously affected by planning and renewal. There is at the same time a rising recognition of the urgency for more competence in the churches as they respond to stimuli and opportunities in community change.

6. Roman Catholicism still lags way behind Protestantism in its approach to the professional planner, but no religious group has yet phrased with the planner an adequate communication, much less a sufficient dialogue.

One of the religious leaders at the fiftieth saw the general objective of planning as "the proper ordering of society so that man might achieve his greatest fulfillment." There were, indeed, many gods such as this in the planning Areopagus which churchmen recognized. For instance, urban statesman James Rouse remarked, "There is a new revolutionary force abroad which I describe as man's concern for the dignity of man." Veteran planner Harland Bartholomew called for vision: "Planners determine the shape of what men see; what they see determines what they become." There was an insistence on the role of spirit as critically central in planning by University of Chicago theologian Dr. Joseph Sittler from a plenary rostrum on the very first morning of the fiftieth!

In summary, the relating clergyman will recognize in the planner an initial integrity, some hope, and much frustration. Usually the planner is an intense, involved, and quite cosmopolitan individual. He will, inevitably, reflect the inheritance of his pre-planning profession. This will result in as many kinds of planner as there are planning backgrounds. Planners may well be strangers to the organized church. They cannot fail, however, to have noted church-based action in metropolis. They will not be sure, by and large, what religion's role so far in civil rights tells them. They will be less familiar with churchmen working beyond protest, though in community after community this work multiplies. Particularly in the matter of church sponsorship of low income housing, the planner will be aware of at least beginning indications of a practical church urbanism.

Planners have learned the hard way how finite man is, how incapable of instant and total efficiency is the democracy, how accustomed many of the citizens they plan for have become to narrow, brief, what's-in-it-for-me-now perspectives. They will hope to find in religion a source of support for an upward and outward mobility in these perspectives. More and more, as is the relevant churchman, the planner is challenged to leadership and yet condemned if he leads too far out front. If he ever had any illusions, urban events in the last few years have amply demonstrated his own personal incompleteness. He is still not sure if he should correct that incompleteness on the social or the cybernetic side of things. As is the relevant churchman, he is not sure how he fits into politics, how he organizes citizens, who indeed are the feasible poor, how he can create an optimal working relationship with his fellow professionals. He knows he makes sense. He knows the urgency of a quick commonwealth. But he cannot, except in his rare private moments, forget that he is part of an establishment, charged to effect what others decide; he is not a free expert. He needs and will welcome the help of churchmen so long as that help is realistic, patient, positive. He will empathize readily with churchmen who are willing to sweat with him through the difficult, building moments as well as stand beside him when he proclaims high human goals for man in metropolis. Even more, he will welcome the impact of religion on the conscience of society and on the political power structures. If religion is indeed able to move the minds of the men who decide about metropolis, he will be significantly assisted in furthering the conclusions to which his own usually concerned conscience drives him.

As the planner faces ahead into his second half century in the United States, he is caught up in a furious crisis of identity. His neighbors converge on "urbanology." Does such convergence leave planning in a situation where it is, in Perry Norton's phrase, "a fifth wheel which steers" a more and more complicated urban car? Or does it, rather, reduce the profession to a kind of spare wheel in the trunk, hauled out and dusted off only if one of the other wheels fails? What does the revolution of instant urban expectations demand of the planner in an affluent society one-fourth poor and powerfully angry in critical places? As planners move to implement participatory democracy, how do they accommodate the danger that they may be raising grass-roots hopes for goals which cannot or at least cannot soon be reached? If the planner jumps to accept bold, innovative social ideas, on what constituency in metropolis can he rely for continuous support? There are friends of the public schools and friends of the public librarian, but the public planner has few friends; and those he has, are often unorganized or platitudinous. Or is all this changing as the social conscience of the nation changes?

One thing is clear. A great number of responsible men are doing, or immediately proposing to do, importantly sophisticated and increasingly coherent things about metropolis. A great number of responsible men are thinking sophisticated and coherent thoughts about metropolis. How does religion relate? Can religion, as church, spirit and congregant, play a meaningful role in this thinking and doing? Can religion, as institution, play a role in "the secular city"?

At AIP's fiftieth anniversary, Alan Altshuler said that an institution is two things. It is "formal organizational arrangements." It is "customary, but well-entrenched modes of thought." Can we in the churches at the same time announce a new relevance, break out from old thought patterns and harness that relevance into new structures? Again, the answer must be developed in the variables of competence, coherence, contact. We shall have to know continuously what is going on, what is doing, what is daring in metropolis. We shall have to systematize our resources and communicate our experiments. We shall need to come to the plans and the planners in metropolis with a great strength of understanding, with a ready sweat as well as with a willing spirit.

It was more than evident at the fiftieth anniversary that, while the naked shrill courage of the prophet and the rights picket remain essential in our as yet inadequate society, it will take more than courage and tocsins to re-make metropolis. "The field," said veteran houser Charles Abrams at the anniversary conference, "requires people who have a grasp of multiple disciplines . . . plus a large gift of common sense." Or, as Gunnar Myrdal put it to the same conference,

"What we need today is not a deceptive hopefulness that success comes easy, but the will to grapple with staggering difficulties." The institution, in short, and the people who decide in institutions require reformation and re-direction. Perhaps Kevin Lynch put the case for this kind of new institutionalism best when he addressed the fiftieth on October 5, 1967: "Experimentation will have to be undertaken with gingerly care. The risk is high and the period of fruition uncertain. Yet this is a most effective way of keeping our future options open. The combination of risk, requirements, and importance means that this work must be institutionalized." There is surely place in the dialogue between institution and society for an expanding interaction between churchman and planner.

On the first day of the 1967 summer Conference on Science for Clergyman at Oak Ridge National Laboratory, Tennessee, Rev. William G. Pollard, Episcopal clergyman and atomic scientist, made this prediction: "I foresee a great religious renaissance. Once the world has adapted to the concept of itself as a spaceship, wondering along the lines of fundamental questions will begin. Mankind in the 20th century is too bedazzled by scientific discoveries for spiritual inquiry."

Hobbes had suggested much earlier that philosophy is leisure's child. Plato, even earlier, has proposed, though his method was unjust, that men could indeed think great thoughts about society only when they were freed from the pedestrian affairs of life. I am not sure the Pollard assessment is correct. I am not at all sure that more leisure will result in more wisdom, either celestial or terrestrial. Indeed, Sebastian de Graza told the fiftieth anniversary conference that, though at times "some form of religious revival" follows a revolution in work habits, a shortening of the labor requirement in our society could rather "bring on the restless tick of boredom, idleness, immorality and increased personal violence."

Freedom from hackwork will not automatically release great flights of human concentration on the taller, more fundamental questions of man's place in time and space. Nevertheless, if such flights are to happen, spirit must be increasingly active with technology in our time. The world of comfortable brothers which the technocrats at Oak Ridge envision will not just happen. The world of golden leisure with a renewed mankind which Fathers Teilhard de Chardin and Pollard seem to suggest will not just happen. It must, in both instances, be planned for, prayed for, sweated out. It is here, principally, that planning and religion converge. The dialogue between churchmen and planners should be one of the most natural conversations in metropolis. It could become for metropolitan man one of the most important.

General Plan
for an Urban Church

FOUR

It is not enough to put up churches or even to create parish center. It is the pastoral effort as a whole which must be adapted to a new situation which concerns all the parishes.[1]

In November, 1965, Lawrence Cardinal Shehan commissioned a professional planning study of the Church in Baltimore, Maryland. Two years later the study was completed and published. It represents in some ways fulfillment of many of the ideas in this book.

Why such a study? There were a number of reasons. One certainly was Cardinal Shehan's concern for the development of new unities of outlook and structure within the Church. He told the National Conference of Catholic Charities in New York on September 24, 1960:

[1] Papal Message on *Urbanization*, signed by Amleto Cardinal Cicognani, to the Semaine Sociale at Bordeaux, France, Summer, 1965.

We must learn to look upon our programs as parts of one integral whole; for, while each is aimed to meet its own special need, all are concerned with the whole problem of Catholic community life. . . . Coordination is not something which is achieved once and for all; it is a continuing process which never ends.[2]

Another reason was an increasing number of parish plant problems in downtown Baltimore. This reason was evident from the fact that negotiations toward engagement of a professional study staff were handled through Archdiocesan Building Commission executives. Other reasons were less local, but equally pertinent. In a time of break and remake the Church must ponder her civics as well as her soul. This requires a procedural as well as a substantive reflection. *Ecclesiam Suam* put it thus: "It is a duty today for the Church . . . to determine the best means for making more immediate, more efficacious and more beneficial her contacts with mankind to which she belongs."[3] In its *Constitution on the Church in the Modern World*, Vatican II added: "The more that both [i.e., church and political community] foster sounder cooperation between themselves . . . the more effective will their service be exercised for the good of all." Finally, it had become more and more certain in Baltimore, as everywhere in a thinking religion, that involvement in metropolis can not be a sometime practical thing. Involvement had to be comprehensive: "Metropolitan mission is not one among many tasks of the presbytery. All instruments of the presbytery should be designed for the performance

---

[2]Address to the Conference by the then Bishop Shehan of Bridgeport, Connecticut.
[3]NCWC Edition (August 6, 1964), par. 18.

of this central task."[4] If this is true in practice, it must also be true in analysis prior to and concurrent with practice:

The interdisciplinary approach, far from being a luxury or a pastime for intellectual dilettantes, belongs at the base of things. It belongs at the very heart of on-going research and development activity as much for relevant religion as for government.[5]

The study thus fell clearly within the mainstream of contemporary local and national Church concern.

Supervising the study in the name of Cardinal Shehan were Auxiliary Bishop T. Austin Murphy, the Right Reverend Monsignor Joseph M. Nelligan, Vicar-General of the Archdiocese, and the late Right Reverend Monsignor Joseph J. Leary, then Chairman of the Archdiocesan Building Commission.

Selection of the study staff was my responsibility. I chose two assistants. Each had a long record of responsible involvement in Baltimore. They were the Very Rev. William J. Lee, S.S., now Rector of St. Mary's Seminary and University, Paca Street, Baltimore. He holds a doctorate in economics from the Catholic University of America and was, at the time of his appointment, an executive member of the Archdiocesan Inner City Committee and a vice-president of the Baltimore Citizen Planning and Housing Association. I also chose Mr. Wood, who had authored

---

[4]*Guidelines for Development of Strategy in Metropolitan Mission.* Board of National Missions, United Presbyterian Church in the United States of America, 475 Riverside Drive, New York City, 10027 (September, 1967), p. 14.

[5]Robert Howes, in *The Church in the Changing City*, L. J. Luzbetak, editor (Techny, Illinois: Divine Word Publications, 1966), p. 197.

major Community Renewal Plan studies in Baltimore and in Providence, Rhode Island. Mr. Wood and I hold Master in City Planning degrees from the Massachusetts Institute of Technology and are Associates in the American Institute of Planners.

A third member of the staff was Mr. Lawrence D. Cook who holds a Master's degree in Architecture from the Catholic University of America, and is a practicing architect in Washington, D.C. Mr. Jack Ladd Carr, with a Master's degree in Planning from the University of Pennsylvania and an Associate in the American Institute of Planners, joined the staff in October, 1966, when he became Director of the study-recommended Archdiocesan Office of Planning and Development. Mr. Carr had been, most recently, Director of Planning at Annapolis, Maryland. Assisting the staff were Mr. Eugene Butler, MCRP, from the Catholic University of America and the Reverend John J. McKenzie, O.S.A., MCE, from the Catholic University of America and graduate student in Planning at the University of Pennsylvania. In short, the staff represented a creative assembly of different viewpoints, scholastic backgrounds, experiences, and professional talents. That it was able to combine these differences in one plan is in itself an achievement.

The area assigned for study covered most of Baltimore. It did not extend beyond the city, but it had to be assessed as part of a metropolitan region. The usual criteria determined its boundaries:

1. client preference;
2. existing client territorial decisions (i.e., parish lines);
3. such areal delineations as had already been established by "social" and "physical" planning agencies in Baltimore. In the study area, there were fifty-two parishes (one

since closed) and forty-one parochial schools. Living in the area were 671,402 people, slightly over seventy percent of the total population of Baltimore. Of these, fifty-two percent (349,968) were white, and forty-eight percent (321,-434) were non-white. To facilitate analysis, four sub-sectors were established. In the East sub-sector there were nine parishes; in the Inner City (further subdivided into Central, Eastern, and Western) there were twenty-five parishes; in the Northwest, ten; in the South, nine.

Initially we had to survey the circumstances. Our data gathering had to be both civil and ecclesiastical. The Baltimore Archdiocese was English North America's first Roman Catholic diocese and its first archdiocese. From its ample original territory most of the dioceses in the United States have been carved. Through long and critical years, its Sulpician Seminaries, St. Mary's and St. Charles', educated priests whose services spanned the nation. Its plenary councils reached the earliest American Church decisions, made the basic local Church laws, produced the classic catechism. Its Cardinal was the founding patriarch of the Catholic University of America. In Baltimore, as so often elsewhere, Catholicism multiplied with immigration. First came the Irish, then the Germans, Poles, Bohemians, Italians, and others. As ethnic neighborhoods grew, so did the Church. Notably assisted by the Third Baltimore Council's mandate to bishops to locate a school near every church, such neighborhoods became firm and enduring through prolific generations. Of the twenty-one parishes in Baltimore in 1877, five were German or Bohemian. A number of parishes were strongly identified with Irish-Americans. The Health and Welfare Council of the Baltimore Area summed it up well. "Church-centered neighborhoods involving particular nationality groups appear to be among the strongest and most readily distinguishable neighborhoods characteristic of early Baltimore."[6] In the same year of 1877, the Archdiocese of Baltimore had 286 regular and archdiocesan priests. There were 210,000 Catholics, and 66 parochial schools. Today in a smaller land area, the archdiocese numbers some 800 regular and archdiocesan priests, serves more than 500,000 Catholics, and has 113 parochial elementary and more than 30 secondary schools.

The Negro apostolate has long been a subject of special concern in Baltimore. In 1829, a religious community of Negro women, the Oblate Sisters of Providence, was founded in Baltimore by the Reverend Nicholas Joubert, S.S., from the Seminary of St. Mary. In 1871, responding to a request from the Second Baltimore Council, four English Mill Hill priests were sent by the Pope to work among American Negroes. On their arrival in Baltimore, these priests staffed St. Francis Xavier Parish. Later, an American Order, the St. Joseph Society of the Sacred Heart (the Josephites), continued this ministry to the Negro, in Baltimore and throughout the South. There are currently five parishes in Baltimore which are staffed by the Society. In these, parishioners are mostly Negro.

If its Church experience has been unusual, the urban experience of Baltimore has been fairly typical of American East Coast cities. Baltimore is part of the southern anchor of East Coast megalopolis. With Washington, D.C., it is one of the fastest growing urban areas in the United States today. There were 1,405,000 people in the Baltimore Stan-

[6]November, 1964.

dard Statistical Area in 1950, 1,727,000 in 1960. If one fact stands out about Baltimore, it is the unusual number of remedial efforts which have been focused on it over the years. Today it ranks among the most researched cities in the United States. From Fight-Blight[7] to the Charles Center, and the highway design team concept, it has been exhaustively studied. Among the latest comprehensive efforts are its Community Renewal Plan and its Model Cities proposal. Availability of these studies was of great help to us. They also indicated a healthy climate of urban concern, at least among the community's leaders.

In the fall of 1965, Baltimore stood between depression and hope. Its housing was mixed. While 43 percent of its 7,247 residential blocks were census-rated "good" in 1960, 47 percent of its blocks in the inner city were now census-rated "poor." It had its show areas. Exciting new construction was underway downtown. Grand proposals for a new Inner Harbor complex which would stretch the Central Business District and the Charles Center westward were announced. There were prospects for subway mass transit. In many parts of the city shiny white steps and stone fronts testified to a pride of ownership which has become a kind of Baltimore trademark. But huge acreages of heavy industry cut into its chance for a totally attractive downtown situation. There were large areas of public housing. Downtown traffic movement was difficult. We faced a record of boldness in some places in dealing with integration, turmoil, and violence; in other areas, nothing had been

---

[7]For Further details, see pages 1-91 of *The Human Side of Urban Renewal*, Millspaugh, Martin and Breckenfeld, Gurney, Fight-Blight, Inc. (Baltimore, Maryland, 1958).

done. Like most East Coast cities, Baltimore was alert to
the urgency of urban improvement. It had a number of
good urban specialists on its planning and renewal staff.
Some top consultants concentrated on its problems. Yet it
was fretted by provincialism and prejudice, somewhat the
prisoner of an unorganized past. No one could doubt that
the word for Baltimore in the middle sixties was crisis,
both danger and opportunity.

From this initial survey, we moved to graphics to illus-
trate problems and possibilities. We prepared a large base
map of the study area. On it, we pin-pointed each parish
and each archdiocesan facility. We then drew up four
overlays, or translucent sheets of the same dimension as
our base map. The first of these located existing and probable urban renewal projects. Each project was colored in
terms of type of renewal, in existence or proposed. The
second overlay located existing and probable public housing projects. Again, these were type-colored. The third
located existing and probable road and transit projects. The
fourth divided the study area in terms of plotted indices
of socio-economic deficiency.

In our first working session with Cardinal Shehan we
placed these overlays consecutively and then together on
the base map. Immediately relationships were indicated
and sequences suggested themselves. Immediately it was
clear that, however pressing the local problems which
called us to Baltimore were, their solution had to be part
of an overall assessment. There could be no question after
that first working session that urban renewal, public housing, and transport change faced the Archdiocese of Baltimore with challenges and choices which had to be estimated generally before responsible particular actions could be

suggested. We could not, of course, ignore the need for specifics. But we had mainly to concentrate on the creation of a pattern, a habit of effective, positive intervention in and response to metropolitan change. This pattern had to be capable of adjustment to alterations in the shape and scope of change in the Church as well as in the community.

Once we had come to this early decision, we discovered almost immediately a curious dilemma. Had we been other than city planners engaged in a planning study, we might have gone at it somewhat differently. As it was, none of us questioned how we should respond to the dilemma. Put simply, the question was one of establishmentarianism! We were in total agreement, as was the client, that the situation required a close re-assessment of Church structures and procedures. Was this wise? Would reform of structures derogate from the new revolutionary spirit blowing in the Church? Emphasizing the institution, would we not constrict the charismatic people? We were well aware, of course, that institutionalism had been distinctly harmful to religion in the past. The record of empire-building, bureaucratic inertia, structured pettiness in some central Church operations was too obvious to ignore. "Intransigence of the structures," as Father Bernard Häring puts it, can most certainly produce a hardening of the arteries of communication and control. Institutionalism can hinder the pulsing of innovative blood through any idea, even through spirit. Far from denying the need for our effort in Baltimore, however, past failures seemed even more insistently to require it. The fault lay not with the existence of arteries and blood. The fault lay with the constriction of those arteries and the obstruction of that blood. Once the worn, weary ways had been swept away, the Church as institution could become fully vital again. A renewed institution could fund, sustain, share, communicate, and assure the continuing thrust of those unstructured experiments which are so necessary to aggiornamento. Daniel Callahan puts it well:

> The question is not whether the churches should be institutionalized, but where they should direct their efforts. A self-serving institutionalism is worthy of condemnation, but an institutionalism that is directed toward the service of society need not be at all reprehensible. If the latter were a response to the organizational exigencies of contemporary society rather than an exercise in narcissism, the bad connotations of "ecclesiastical institutionalism" could easily drop away. The churches should be so structured that their aspiration to service is matched by a sophistication and outer-directed organizational apparatus sufficient to realize their desires.[8]

As to how decisions ought to be made within the Church as institution, this was not really our problem. We had to recognize a debate in practice and in theory as to how decisions should be reached and by whom. Our problem was simply to provide a system, an organized series of relationships which could serve religion with equal effectiveness whatever the outcome of the decision-making debate. Whoever "called the shots" in the Baltimore Church twenty years from the time our study was done would require a mechanism to support and implement his decisions. He would also require a resource of information and information analysis and a habitual coordination among his

---

[8]Daniel Callahan, "The Quest for Social Relevance" in *Daedalus*, Vol. 96, No. 1 (Winter, 1967) of the Proceedings of the American Academy of Arts and Sciences, p. 162.

local and central agencies. It was our task to provide this kind of service. In doing so, we were in no way suggesting that other things would not be happening in the Baltimore Church through the single zeal of single congregants, and quite outside any structured arrangement.

We had no illusions as we started in Baltimore that nothing had been done prior to our arrival. In fact, the Baltimore Church was in significant part a thinking church. A number of individual priests and laymen had already demonstrated strong civic concern. It did seem, however, that there was need for a new unity of effort and for a much improved totality of concern. We stood somewhat as Abbe Michonneau twenty years before had stood in his Paris parish: "We only want to bring together ideas that are now scattered and unable to express themselves."[9] Out of the observations and experiences we brought together in the Baltimore study, three general goals emerged early. Each called for new maturity in the Church approach to the community. Each, while in a sense a catch word, summed up exactly the sense of what we hoped to accomplish.

The first general goal was *coherence*. The dictionary (Webster's Third New International) defines coherence as "systematic or methodical connectedness or interrelatedness, especially when governed by logical principles." In both its staff, that is, its central and topical agencies, and in its line, that is its local and particular operating agencies, the Church in Baltimore required a new connectedness. The complexity and the seriousness of problems in metropolis demanded this. Coherence had to be a matter of policy as well as a matter of organization.

[9]Abbe G. Michonneau, *Revolution in a City Parish*, p. xix.

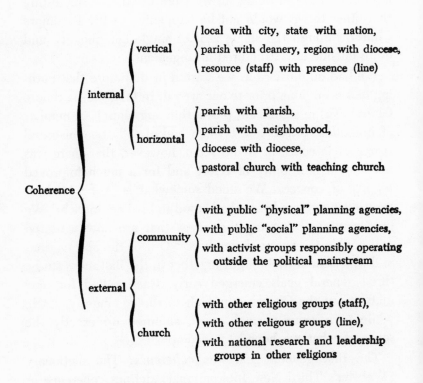

Within itself, the Church must link up its offices and officials to deal from a habitually inter-office base with inter-disciplinary problems. Linkages have to be developed with community planning, renewal, and fight poverty agencies. New, firm linkages are essential between the religious groups in metropolis. Linkages in this category replace an earlier randomness, though, of course, they can never eliminate the need and the value of personal action by single congregants. What is required is a constant, informed, and united presence of spirit in city. There are no Protestant slums. There is no Roman Catholic urban renewal. There is no Jewish model city. Each of these is an interfaith challenge and an interfaith chance. Happily, coherence begins to happen within the Church and among the churches with greater frequency, with a new depth of staff, and with more adequate research, though the resource factor is still unsure. There is still a considerable distance to be traveled before a similar kind of coherence is in effect between churchmen and planning agencies.

The second general goal was *competence*. The dictionary (Webster's Third New International) defines competence as "the state of being functionally adequate or of having sufficient knowledge, judgment, skill." Any institution which proposes to shape the psyche and help shape the physique of metropolis must have within itself such an adequacy. Involved in competence are, at least, these factors. There must be a fund of responsible knowledge generally, and accurate information particularly. There must also be a professional ability to judge and recommend in terms of the context in which the institution finds itself. Competence must extend to means as well as to ends. The Church can look in several places for this kind of competence: to its own urban universities, for one, to such national research organizations as the Center for Applied Research in the Apostolate (CARA) for another, to conferences and workshops set up to deal with various aspects of the metropolitan situation, for a third. Competence, however, ought also be located in each urban diocese. Even if it were simply a question of old bricks or new mortar, competence in the diocese about metropolis is essential. What the Church does with its structures and land is vitally important to the community; what the community does with its bull-dozers and its projects is vitally important to the Church. Much more is at stake, of course, but the conclusion remains. If the Church intends to assume a positive relevance in metropolis, it must provide itself with wisdom as well as with goodwill, and this on a permanent basis.

The third general goal was *contact*. The dictionary (Webster's Third New International) defines contact as "a condition of meeting, connecting or communicating." Engineers now speak often of interface. This is the surface along which two physical bodies come together. The word has moved into wider usage, as witness the sign on Catholic University's Chemical Engineering bulletin board: "The Good Engineer Should be Pounding the Interfaces of Knowledge." In any case, a permanent interface must be built between religion and community planning. Change in metropolis is not singular, not simple, not once over lightly! Change happens in multiple dimensions with all kinds of interaction over a very complicated time. Intermittent association with the renewers of metropolis no longer suffices. If the Church loses contact with the change-makers or at least the change-planners, it risks one of several things. It can become hopelessly naive. It can run to rash judgment or rank obstructionism. It may be that at the end of a responsible process of contact with any particular problem, the Church may still opt to oppose it, but at least it will do so from understanding, not from hasty oversimplification. A bridge responsibility like this cannot, of course, be reserved to any one office, but it must begin in one responsible place. In that place, at least, someone must record, overlook, and supplement. Files must be maintained, key meetings attended, strategic approaches undertaken. The urgency of such a contact point multiplies as the Church assumes a more constructive role in a more complex metropolis.

Toward the development of these three goals, we directed a number of specific recommendations. The first, and fundamental, recommendation called for an Archdiocesan Office for Planning and Development (APD), headed by a professional planner and a professional social worker with a strong specialty in community organization. What we wanted was a working duality at the center, a duality of competence and contact. What we hoped was that by placing two individuals in tandem, both the "physical" and "social" contexts of religion in metropolis could be developed and then interrelated in one coherent program.

We recommend this scope of services for APD:

I. ANNUAL REPORT. Clearly, with unmistakable action-outline and appropriate annotation, this report will constitute a yearly retrospective and prospective overview of the situation of the Church in Baltimore. Its particular categories will include the following:

1. The current state of community change and planning in the Baltimore Metropolitan Area. Important studies and project proposals, addresses, maps, and documents will be appended to those copies of the report forwarded to key archdiocesan decision-makers. These will be indexed and abstracted to permit easy analysis and retrieval.

2. Proposals for substantive Church response to current planning and renewal activity in the Baltimore Metropolitan Area, with specific indications of the type of action required and how it ought to be staged.

3. Definition of principal problems and possibilities in Church land and plant relation to the changing development of the Baltimore Metropolitan Area. This includes both priorities and state of project reports.

4. Summary, or inclusion in full, as seems necessary, of special spot studies made by APD in the preceding year.

5. Status of the Capital Improvement Program.

The report will vary in detail as the urgency of each item may require. Its distribution will be as the archdiocese determines. It may be well, where certain executive discretion is required, to prepare summary versions of the Report for public distribution and comment.

II. CAPITAL IMPROVEMENT PROGRAM. Every six years, APD will prepare a detailed Capital Improvement Program for the Church in the Baltimore Metropolitan Area. This will apply to land, plant, and other facility expenditures. It will be prepared in consultation with relevant Church agencies and individuals and will be a principal consultative function of the Planning and Development Advisory Council. This Program will suggest priorities. Each year's Annual Report of APD will measure the accomplishment of this Capital Improvement Program as modified and accepted or altered by archdiocesan decision-makers and will propose amendments to it as required.

III. MANDATORY REFERRAL. It is critical that APD operate in an annual review and overall capacity. It must also be conversant with and pre-advised of prospective changes in land and plant use on the part of other Church agencies, local and central. Just as in a well-planned community the planning office is asked to give written comment on all proposals for important alterations in land patterns, so proposals for major change, for disposal and acquisition of Church land as well as for significant Church response to civic projects, must be referred to APD for written comment prior to activation. What is at stake here is the urgency of reflection on each single proposal in terms of the state of metropolis. It is simply not sufficient, either in Church or city hall, for the planning office to speak only in end-of-the-year generalisms. APD's role in mandatory referral is not to countermand, obstruct, or pre-empt responsible action by other Church agencies. It is meant to provide Church decision-makers with a professional judgment on the particular proposal, based on APD's overall familiarity with plans, programs, and likely possibilities in metropolitan change. Other variables may enter into the decision-maker's ultimate election, but at least a reasoned overview will be before him when he makes this election.

IV. ECUMENICAL CIVICS. I coined this term some years ago to express my thinking in the matter of interfaith community action. It says quite simply that, while the personal, particular type of community involvement which some clergy in some places practiced in some issues has its validity and is important, it no longer suffices. What is required is a structured, staffed, informed metropolitan presence by the several religions of a community united to promote commonwealth. The basis of ecumenical civics is emphatically not self-advancement. There will be occasions when churches together must reflect on plant problems, apportionment of religious spaces in a renewal area, highway impacts on church property. By and large, however, ecumenical civics is an outgoing effort designed to forge coherent linkages between all involved religions in the community in terms of the civic need. Here APD will assist, catalyze, as well as initiate. In conjunction with the Archdiocesan Commission for Christian Unity and other church agencies, APD will be responsible for promoting effective interfaith community action. It will represent the Church. It will speak itself or collaborate with other Church spokesman in furthering such action. One of its principal charges will be to help give interfaith civic associations a continuous life and purpose and to be itself a chief resource and leadership factor in their evolution.

V. CONTACT AND REPRESENTATION. One of APD's most critical responsibilities is to function as a bridge between community and Church. It will maintain a permanent liaison with key community offices, citizens, and activists. Its library must be constantly current. At the same time it will be the voice of the Church informing the community of the Church's attitude on various aspects of metropolitan change. Where such a statement is deemed appropriate by archdiocesan decision-makers, for instance, APD will speak for the Church in zoning, urban renewal, housing, and highway development.

VI. SPOT STUDIES. APD will undertake such studies as the archdiocesan decision-makers may require of particular problems in the Baltimore Metropolitan Area.

VII. NEW TOWNS. In the course of the study which led to the Baltimore Urban Parish Report, and at the specific suggestion of its director, Cardinal Shehan moved to enter ecumenical activities at Columbia New Town, Maryland. What has happened subsequently has amply demonstrated the validity of these activities. APD, in cooperation with the developers, with other Church agencies and other churches, will be the principal technical representative of the Church in its relations with Columbia and with similar ventures as they occur. On the basis of lessons learned at and from Columbia, APD will be able to record the progress of ecumenical activities there and to communicate them as requested.

In close connective sequence with the establishment of APD, we next recommended a kind of advisory board of directors for the planning and development operation and a procedure through which central presence could be assured in terms of Church civics in Baltimore. In the first instance, we called for a *Planning and Development Advisory Council* (PDAC). It will consist basically of the four metropolitan advisers to be listed below, plus heads of key archdiocesan agencies. Here again, we could not be sure just how the entire issue of decision-making in the Church would be resolved. It may well be that membership in PDAC should include representatives of parish councils, priests' senates and associations, and other concerned laity. The problem is, of course, to keep numbers small enough to be efficient, large enough to be comprehensive in terms of representation. A second problem was to involve with APD a working group of key Church people, but not to hamstring the professionals with an over-riding decisive power. We provided for an advisory body through which operating agencies, when charged later to implement various sections of APD's Annual Report, would already have been familiar with the process out of which these sections emerged. At the same time, PDAC could provide a very valuable sounding board and comprehensive resource for APD. Particularly, we saw PDAC's role as advisory in the preparation of APD's Annual Report.

In the second instance, we called for a *regionalization of Church direction and action in the Baltimore Metropolitan Area.* Rather than go through what seemed to us the unnecessary process of creating new "urban deans," we suggested a similar approach through the naming of four metropolitan advisers. We divided the City of Baltimore and the next outward ring of suburban communities around it into four sectors. One sector, to be headed by the Director of the Archdiocesan Urban Commission functioning as its metropolitan adviser, was the Inner City. The other three were drawn to represent pie-shaped land areas. Metropolitan advisers could be either lay or clerical. Their task would be to help provide for a new coherence and communication on a level as between parish and diocese, neighborhood and community, suburb and city. They would also begin to provide for a regional sharing and detailing of Church concern for community, as well as for a feedback from each sector to responsible central offices, particularly to APD. The scope of services for each of the metropolitan advisers would include:

1. membership on the Archdiocesan Planning and Development Advisory Council;

2. public representation of the Archdiocese within his sector, this in consultation with APD and other relevant Church agencies;

3. convocation and support of civic educational programs within his sector.

While the metropolitan adviser who is Director of the Archdiocesan Urban Commission will serve full-time in view of the peculiar urgency of his situation, the three other advisers will serve part-time. As the Church in Baltimore wrestles with the idea of episcopal vicars, parish councils, and other methods for widening authority outward from the archdiocesan building, it is quite possible that adjustments may be required in the implementation of this recommendation. The logic of it remains.

Final central recommendations dealt with three archdiocesan agencies.

1. *The Urban Commission.* During the course of the study the relatively informal "Inner City Office" of the Archdiocese was replaced by a full-fledged, permanently staffed Archdiocesan Urban Commission. This replacement was clearly more than a change in name. It occurred without any prior knowledge or advice from the study staff. Had we had the opportunity, as ought to have been the case within our mandate, I am not sure just how we would have recommended. The point that concerned us, of course, was precisely what the relationship of the Urban Commission to APD should be. We deliberated at some length on this item. In the end we suggested that the Urban Commission, as all other central agencies, should operate within the general context of APD. We saw for it a very valuable role in education and action in the area of race relations and in representing a territorial concentration of downtown parishes. Its director will serve on the Planning and Development Advisory Council as a metropolitan adviser.

2. *Associated Catholic Charities.* Charities has a long record of involvement with urban poverty. This is both a local and a national fact. Increasingly, involvement seems

to demand community organization as well as the traditional social welfare casework. We recommended that Charities be a principal partner in a habitual, inter-agency Church response to poverty in Baltimore. Such a partnership would require a thorough reexamination of previous unitary policies as well as, quite possibly, new structures and new personnel. The critical point was to recognize and capitalize on Charities in the development of an integrated Church resource.

3. *Education.* We found ourselves in a real quandary here. In fact, we deliberately postponed any recommendations in this area until the end of the study. In many of the matters in which he is asked to plan, the planner is not himself an expert. But usually he can discover a consensus of contemporary thinking or can engage sub-consultants who will advise him on the state of the matter. Catholic education remains in a condition of furious debate. There is no consensus, no state. Of several things we were sure. Nationally and locally research was underway on the financial and substantive future of Catholic education. There was not the slightest indication that the decision-makers in Baltimore intended to truncate, much less eliminate, Catholic secondary education. We were sure, finally, that despite certain differences of responsibility and clientele, no justification could be found for a continued fragmentation in the Church's educational activity. Our initial recommendation, then, called for a combination in one office of all this activity. Specifically, we proposed that the Confraternity of Christian Doctrine, the Newman Apostolate, parochial school administration be united. We did this, aware of the usual problems of personnel and weighting of concentration which arise in any effort to consolidate

previously separate efforts, but even more aware of the validity of pooling time, facilities, funds, and educational staff. In addition to already commissioned research studies in Catholic education in Baltimore, a further research would have to be done. Just how could consolidation most effectively occur without diminishing the net impact of any existing and successful single program? Pending consolidation and completed research, our specific recommendations were rather technical than substantive. It was obvious that educational finance would have to be reconsidered. Somehow resources presumably available elsewhere would have to be brought to bear in hard-pressed downtown schools. We recommended the designation of demonstration parochial schools, as much as possible in conjunction with demonstration parishes. Into these schools there should be directed a special concentration of the best personnel, the best teaching methods, and the latest structural improvements. We recommended a reconsideration of the role of the school in the urban neighborhood in terms of what metropolis today can learn from Clarence Perry's celebrated monograph on the subject.[10] We recommend, finally, exploring with the City of Baltimore the possibility of educational parks in which parochial as well as public schools could be sited. As with Charities, we proposed that Education be a principal partner in the urban relevance of the Church. Just how all of these recommendations could be worked out was a question we suggested for both APD and the new unified Department of Education. Their joint

---

[10]See *The Neighborhood Unit: A Scheme of Arrangement for the Family Life in Community: Vol. VII, Regional Survey of New York and its Environs* (New York City, 1929).

attention to it should be one of the most meaningful consequences of the entire study.

Another matter which required specific recommendation was Church sponsorship of lower income mass housing. Two things were evident. There exist Federal programs which encourage such sponsorship. To date, churches across America have responded only in very limited measure to this challenge, though there has been much talk. During the study, indeed, the nation's Roman Catholic bishops met in Washington and explicitly proposed a widening of church activity in housing. What are the reasons behind the gap between religion's words and religion's deeds? These, in our judgment, are the principal ones:

1. Churches lack competence in real estate market analysis procedures prior to site selection.

2. Churches lack competence in site planning and development.

3. Churches are uncertain as to paper requirements and governmental relationships required to carry a project through from proposition to construction.

4. Churches lack competence in housing management and do not wish to assume landlord relationships.

5. Churches are, quite simply, afraid that by involving themselves with housing they may get stuck with a nonviable financial commitment.

What was required, if this analysis was accurate, was to create some body which could eliminate these blocks. Its charge would be to supply information, inspire confidence, provide managerial, legal, and financial advice and undertake to cut the necessary red tape. We recommended, therefore, that the archdiocese join with other church groups in Baltimore in an interfaith housing advisory corporation. At least one full-time professional staff executive would have to be hired. Communications should be opened with appropriate national organizations, such as Urban America, Inc. Local parishes and/or religious orders could engage the services of the corporation on a fee basis. Their problems and fears would thus be transferred to a competent point in which increasing experience would develop. Interfaith housing efforts in Columbia New City, Maryland, clearly offered an example for guidance.

The Parishes. Through the whole course of the study, we had been visiting parishes and interviewing pastors and parishioners. We were never satisfied that we had talked to enough people. We did make a sufficient survey at least to permit a profile. There were fifty-one parishes altogether. Our central recommendations would affect all of them. What we recommended for each of them was, of course, particular. We need only generalize here.

The parish itself is still the known microcosm of religion. It remains, for all its change, the visible presence of the great big Church in this here and now neighborhood. How and what happens to it is critical. It has even been somewhat facetiously suggested that while a Christian takes his platitudes from his Church generally, he takes his attitudes from his parish.

As our parochial inquiries progressed, we discovered a wide diversity of outlook. Stuctures varied, but so did spirits. In some cases we encountered a heavy inertia; in others, a settled despair. There was a high optimism count here and there, but there was also frequently a skepticism about urban possibilities on the one hand or the chance for effective Church action to develop such possibilities on the other hand.

Two perplexities recurred: a perplexity about how to support continued parochial activities as congregations shift away, and a perplexity about how to relate to what the community seems about to do in the shadow of the parish spires. There was another perplexity, somewhat beyond the mind of most pastors and parishioners, but important nonetheless. This was a perplexity about parish form. What type of local presence will best accommodate a post-Vatican II religion? Should we recommend strengthening the large urban parish, opting for pontifical liturgies, uniting congregants across color and economic lines before common altars? Should we rather propose floating ministries to new non-territorial communities? Should the move be rather toward missions, store-front activity for evangelism, pre-evangelism, and post-evangelism? If downtown Baltimore becomes a strange emulsion of the high-rise affluent and near affluent and the high-rise poor, what ought the Church's parochial response be? We could not, as planners, resolve these questions. We did recommend at least that each section of Baltimore should be responsibly covered by a parochial presence. We did recommend that the new resource, overview, and leadership activity we were suggesting at the archdiocesan level would encourage, provide assistance for, and communicate experiments in various types of parochial change. The exact manner of experimentation must rest with the apostolic ingenuity of the priests and people of the archdiocese.

From our profiles for the fifty-one parishes, we came to these general conclusions:

1. The local parish needs and has a right to expect far more effective help from the central Church in the matter of advice, guidance, and support as it moves to be relevant in metropolis. Locally, in Baltimore, our recommendations for APD and metropolitan advisers plus the whole element of new competences, new contacts, and new coherences at the Catholic Center should contribute to provide this expanded help.

2. Personnel practices are a critical key to a more adequate parochial relevance. From seminary on, the clergy of metropolis require a continued familiarity with urbanism, a sense of pastoral teamwork, and encouragement toward responsible socio-economic initiative. This means preparation prior to ordination, continuing education after.

3. A new community awareness, habitual contact with the neighborhood, and facilities for developing programs from this awareness and contact are imperative in most urban parishes. Even where remarkable starts have already been made, there is need for much more.

4. The parish, as canon law envisions it, exists for all the people in its area, not just for its congregants. If, however, parishes are to function on this comprehensive scale, somehow additional financial resources will have to be pumped into those parishes which simply cannot survive on revenue from the few congregants who remain to them. Multi-purpose inner city parochial schools, social workers in blighted parish areas, rehabilitated parochial structures, experiments in neighborhoods which cannot indigenously support such experiments—all demand new or at least differently allocated financing. Many of our recommendations had to be tagged with a dollar sign. At least, they required a notable retrenchment of plan and a notable shifting of

dollars from one place to another. One pastor, sitting in his slum parlor, told us, "I have to be concerned for my people and available to them whether the problem is bats in the belfry or rats in the basement." This concern begins on a counseling level, but to be effective it must go further. If the Church is to widen its involvement at the neighborhood level and be housed in a newly effective plant, money is essential—and fairly big money! We could never be sure just how this added resource was to be found or with what degree of practical success this kind of shifting could be effected.

As with all urban plans, success can be measured only over time. The recommendations of the plan must be activated in whole or in part before a final judgment can be made on it. Personalities have to be fed into the proposed system, altering it for better or for worse. Its worth must be tested partly by its ability to adjust to meet unforeseen change.

Our general plan for the urban Church in Baltimore will be much affected by the Church's own developing idea of itself and by experimentation nationally and locally with collective Church practices. Perhaps the key question here is the same question which must be asked of any urban plan: To what continuous extent has it shaped the overall institutional policy, assisted it in its associational civics, and influenced into a staged coherence the programs of each operating institutional agent, local and central, staff and line? A second key question, where the plan is private rather than public, must concern the degree to which the plan makes the institution a better citizen of the metropolis in which it locates. That degree is a factor of positive as well as responding responsibility in community change.

Perhaps the Baltimore Urban Parish Study[11] made an important model at a time the Church badly required such a model and set in place several conclusions which merit consideration:

FIRST. The Church, like all other metropolitan institutions, makes a more meaningful intervention in metropolis if it has within itself a resource which can:

1. carefully and coherently assemble data from within and around itself on metropolitan change and its capacity to respond to it;

2. express that data in active form;

3. responsibly analyze the data and regularly report it to decision-makers;

4. propose alternative responses to metropolitan change with such adjustment in church forms and functions as may be required to activate those responses.

SECOND. Somehow the financial resource of the Church must be coupled more continuously into its planned policies through a capital improvement program.

THIRD. Decision-makers in the Church, whoever and however they are, must be provided each year with a professional overview of major problems and possibilities in land, structures, and organization. This overview must be

----

[11]Indicative of early comment on the Baltimore Urban Parish Study was an editorial appearing in *Commonweal*, February 2, 1968 (page 520), which said in part: "The Baltimore Urban Parish Study . . . is a model of intelligent, sensitive thought, surveying and planning. . . . There is a happy absence of pious rhetoric and heavenly visions; the tone is realistic and yet hopeful. . . . How remarkable this kind of specificity is in the American Catholic Church. . . . Particularly impressive are the recommendations made to place the Church in the middle of urban housing renewal."

weighted in terms of importance and immediacy of need and geared into a realistic budget.

FOURTH. A feedback, research, and leadership function must be provided in Church universities, and through national and regional bodies set up specifically for this purpose and adequately funded, where experiences in metropolis can be gathered, analyzed, compared, and communicated.

FIFTH. The problem of personnel training, placement, and management is clearly critical in Church planning for relevance in metropolis.

The Baltimore Urban Parish Study has now entered history as document. It begins its testing time as prelude and invitation to action. If it does nothing else, it suggests a responsible dialogue of preachers and planners. From such a dialogue, the Church, the churches, the planning profession, and metropolitan man himself all stand to benefit! It will be most interesting in twenty years to discover what differences the study and the dialogue have in fact made in Baltimore, the Church, and in Baltimore, the metropolis.

Church University
in Metropolis

FIVE

[The university has a] responsibility to see to it that knowledge and skills which it has developed or assembled . . . can be used to affect urban change and development. . . . The university is part of the larger community. . . . It is conditioned by and, in turn, conditions this larger urban environment.[1]

So far I have dealt with questions within questions. So, too, this subject is blurred by its stance at the intersection of complexities. Neither Church nor university, nor metropolis, itself, is today a sure thing. Combine the three, and unsureness multiplies. Nevertheless, since the Church is university as well as parish and diocese in many urban areas, the subject must be discussed where and as it now seems to be.

---

[1]John Bebout, "Urban Extension: University Services to the Urban Community," *American Behavioral Scientist* (February, 1963), p. 24.

The role of Church as university in metropolis cannot be assessed without first asking several contextual questions. What is the ideal and the potential for university as intervention in metropolis? Can Church-affiliated universities survive with an appreciable Church dimension? Will their churchness, for any one of several reasons, be so reduced as to make them indistinct from their secular neighbors? There are further questions originating in constituency expectation of university. What does metropolis want from its universities? HUD's former Undersecretary Robert C. Wood has said: "The public and the public sector are ready for serious, sustained academic inquiry in urban affairs. Are the academics ready for them?"[2] His point is generally valid, but the fact is by no means so simple. The "public" is not at all unanimous either in its felt collective need for universities or in its readiness to accommodate such service as universities offer it. What does religion want from its universities? Here, too, the situation is confused.

One thing is certain. In our substantively technological and territorially metropolitan society higher education is desperately important.

John Gardner, former Secretary of the Department of Health, Education, and Welfare, has called education "the well-nigh universal ingredient" for the solution of all societal problems. There are several reasons for this. First, as man's option over creation grows, so does the requirement for an informed will and the intricacy of the mechanisms required to express that will. More and more, as the problems become more complex, the solutions more inter-disciplinary,

---

[2]Robert C. Wood, "The University's New Role in Urban Research," address at the meeting of the Association of Urban Universities, Detroit, Michigan, November 6, 1967.

and the commitment to citizen involvement more insistent, there is an urgency for educated men and motives quite beyond any which has existed in the past. There is, second, a great urgency for continuing education in community if the professional citizen is to understand what happens around him with that sophistication of understanding which is essential to responsible citizenship. Add to these factors the widening of educational expectations to include more and more young people over more and more years. Add the requirement for increased skills in an automated work world. Add too the whole notion of systems analysis and systems solution. The subject is not new in these pages. It can be re-phrased here in terms of what Oak Ridge's Alvin M. Weinberg describes as a "coherent doctrine." By this he means "a set of precepts and viewpoints, some from the technological sciences, some from the social sciences, some not from science but rather drawn from common sense and experience, that constitute a rational, integrated approach to the problem."[3] If, indeed, not disparate wisdoms, however excellent in themselves, but coordinated concepts and feedbacks across disciplinary boundaries are necessary, then the university has a clearly critical role in metropolis. If the civic goal must be more and more to inter-relate and systematize practice and theory, then the university can be uniquely helpful in metropolis. It is not the purpose of this book to discuss the future course of American education. Some details must suffice: they establish a giant need.

If the case for a renewed and much widened university commitment to community is compelling, it must not blur

---

[3]Alvin M. Weinberg, "Social Problems and National Socio-Technical Institutions," in *Oak Ridge National Laboratory Review* (Winter, 1968), p. 19.

the possible dangers of hasty, crisis-only action. The university which intelligently relates to the society around it cannot be hurt by such a relationship. Intelligence, however, premises awareness of pitfalls as well as potentials. Intelligence requires that when any institution proposes to weave itself into a pattern of interaction with another institution, it must do so with careful forethought or risk its integrity.

Two polar attitudes are possible as university looks at community.

One pole I describe as either an original innocence or Greek-groves attitudes. Here, and I shall be purposely hyperbolic, the university is a comfortable collection of pipe-smoking, somewhat quaint thinkers, dialoguing with students under sunny olive trees in a place of perpetual peace and no sweat. Here the university returns to what is imaged as a time of original innocence when universities nobly avoided the mess and medley of the world around them. The university, in this dimension, is irrelevant to, supremely indifferent about, and transcendent over calendars and clocks. It unites man across centuries and continents. It shows him his oneness out of the separatenesses which otherwise divide him. The university's constituency becomes the uncommon man who alone has the time and the talent to reorganize the commanalty of mankind. The scholar's contribution to society is not direct involvement in its daily difficulties, but a constant and coherent presence of collective scholarship, enduring spirit, and intellectual hope. It should be added that most Greek grovers look upon "professional" schools as demeaning and essentially alien in the universe of the university. Often, too, more specific aspects of community involvement are considered distracting and trivial. One of the most destructive adjectives in the Greek-grove vocabulary is "applied." It has become, in fact, a one-word weapon. It is used with flailing devastation against any and all tentatives on the part of the university to commit itself in practical extra-university situations. Too eternal to be immediate, the argument runs, the university must be too universal to be particular.

At the second pole is what I describe as the total immersion attitude. It is impatient of all "theory." It demands involvement as a continuum of close and empathetic association as between town and gown. It recognizes no difficulty with relevance. It wants to strip the university as soon as possible of anything and everything which would remove it from "where the action is." It sees such immense benefits from immediacy that it questions the abstract and the general. In its spectrum the university becomes an adjunct of social deciders and a passionate advocate of here and now social reform both through its faculty and its students.

Neither polar position, of course, is just. Each has some merit. Over-involvement, like under-involvement, is an excess in which the metropolitan university indulges at its own and the community's peril. Again, though, since most of these pages are enthusiastic about expanding involvement, it is necessary first to face up to possible pitfalls.

Pitfall number one is this. In accepting a paid commission to serve some organization outside itself, the university could lose its independence of outlook and its integrity of free judgment. He who hires and feeds the fiddler calls the tune. It has been written:

> Institutions will have to become less neutral in the face of pressing social and moral issues and more and more concerned. Northrop Frye, the Canadian critic who has been in

residence at Cornell this spring, has said of scholarship that it is always in danger of degenerating from detachment to indifference . . . Universities, [however], will have to make sure they are not so dependent upon government and business for their survival that they cannot afford to speak out plainly when necessary.[4]

It has also been said: "There is . . . danger . . . that the university may become so involved with predominant community values (or values of particular groups asking assistance) that it might implicitly support and undergird them irrespective of the university's moral position."[5]

Some universities have rejected Federal intelligence funding on the grounds that acceptance would compromise them. Unless it is carefully hedged with assurances of freedom, contractual engagement of the university to service one metropolitan agency or constituency could create real problems for responsible scholarship.

Pitfall number two is this. Too close a concentration on the details of an immediate, proximate situation could reduce the university's potential to contribute a broad, thoughtful, and long-range wisdom to the solution of the problems of metropolis. There are at least two aspects of this pitfall. Harvard's Dr. Pusey has indicated one: "Learning is apt to be most useful, even with professional schools, when it does not aim too intently or too directly at the goals of immediate utility."[6]

---

[4]Dr. James E. Perkins, President of Cornell University, "Commencement Address," Notre Dame University, June, 1968.
[5]"Ecumenical Strategy in the Academic World," Report of the World Student Christian Fellowship, Bossey, Switzerland, May, 1964.
[6]Nathan M. Pusey, address at the University of California, September 26, 1959.

A second aspect revolves around the necessity, as one descends from the general to the particular, of making specific decisions about immediate issues. In urging new urban extension activity on the part of the university in metropolis, Kirk R. Petshek warns "those concerned" to "keep their eyes on the sparrow of concern for the benefit of all members of the metropolitan area, not only a municipality, or one or two neighborhoods, or even a few blocks."[7]

To be involved as an institution with a metropolitan neighborhood in crisis will often require the university to make some extremely difficult decisions. If the neighborhood is in crisis, this means among other things that some issue is before it which is emotionally charged and in which the bulk of the university's neighbors have opted already for one side. There is a range of such issues, but conflicts over public housing location and freeway routing suggest themselves as most likely. Suppose a university's near neighborhood leaders have decided to fight a freeway proposed to run through the area. Suppose they have galvanized their fellow citizens through several stages of opposition into a vociferous and noisy intransigence. Suppose they have linked up with similar negatives across the city in a shouting, floor-stamping, all-out resistance to freeways generally. While all this is going on, and I suggest no ethical judgment whatsoever on the course of events, suppose the university announces it is now ready and eager for a new relevance in and with the neighborhood around it. Inescapably, the neighbors will want to know just what the university's position is on the

---

[7]Kirk R. Petshek, "A New Role for City Universities—Urban Extension Programs," in *Journal of the American Institute of Planners* (November, 1964), p. 312.

questionable freeway. The university can respond to this question in one of several ways. It can say nothing. But such a reticence will be interpreted by the neighbors as directly contradictory of its new relevance and, most probably, as connivance with the pro-freeway establishment. It can do nothing collectively but permit and/or encourage individual students and faculty to take sides. But even this, if it becomes sizable, will be interpreted as formal university commitment. Suppose, however, the university does decide to assume an official position. If the position is platitudinous, it will be safe, but it will satisfy no one. If, however erudite its sentences, it comes down on one side of the issue or the other, the problem remains. Suppose it coincides with the attitude of its fight-freeway neighbors. It will be accepted and applauded. It will have reduced the psychic distance between it and those who have mobilized the neighbors. It will be hailed as helpful and committed. It can count for a while at least on much proximate goodwill.

But suppose this is not the case. Suppose the university polls those in its faculty who are most familiar in their professional competences with freeways and with metropolis, and the result of this poll is a suggestion that the university endorse the freeway as minimally disruptive of people and important for the metropolis as a whole. Then what? What does the university do? The situation has long since polarized. If the university announces for the freeway, it risks loss of community empathy at a critical juncture. It risks, even more seriously, a traumatic conflict from which even years may not be sufficient for recovery. It opens itself to charges of venal self-interest. It will be pilloried in the arenas of gossip and rumor. If it rejects its own experts, on the other hand, it will be applauded by its noisy neighbors, but it will hurt its constructive image in the community as a whole and it will most certainly compromise its academic integrity. Perhaps the freeway illustration puts the question rather more simply than it will usually happen. The point remains. The university must be a jealously free partner if and as it enters neighborhood civics. Yet it cannot ignore the facts of political psychology.

Pitfall number three also poses problems. The university intervening as an institution in metropolis cannot overlook the sheer reality of its own institutional interests. In theory, of course, what is best for the whole is best for the part. In practice, at least as they are understood and fought over by real men in a real world, the interest of the university and the interest of the community in which it is located can and do diverge at important points. So long as the university talks principle and catalyzes commonwealth, fine. But if and as it puts (or seems to put) its weight behind or against a specific course of civic action, its own institutional interest must be a critical variable in the decision to do so. The record of town-gown conflict in Madison, Wisconsin, for instance, and Chicago, Illinois, and West Philadelphia, Pennsylvania, is ample enough to suggest difficulties even on the presumption that in each case the involved university acted with great foresight and generous vision when it intervened in its environs. Suppose we continue to indulge this happy presumption. The university wants and tries to be a good neighbor. It wants to stay locationally and influentially central in metropolis. Its space-structures-and-access requirements, however, may suggest support for certain projects which its neighbors, rightly or wrongly, oppose. What then?

Too easily, in this event, the university can become a powerful, impersonal, malevolent presence fighting the rights of "people." Against the University of Pennsylvania's involvement with change in her neighborhood, West Philadelphia's Mrs. Hattie Humphrey put her case:

> You talk about what an enlightened university could do. A university cannot be enlightened, only a human being can. . . . Social utility for the present residents of university (urban renewal) Area III is diametrically opposed to social utility for the institution and the university type man who will inhabit this community.[8]

By the very nature of its physical form and requirement, it is all too simple for its critics to image the urban university as an enemy of those whose residences its expansion pattern threatens. It is difficult to see how, even with maximum wisdom, the university can fully avoid this pitfall.

Pitfall number four is this: Involvement in metropolis today means more than careful research, erudite editorials, and polysyllabic discussion in faculty lounges. All these continue to be important, and in certain circumstances a university may perhaps satisfy community expectations by a combination of them. For this generation, however, involvement is charging into situations with the flaming sword of righteousness, not just preaching prudence. Furious polarizations now clobber our social conscience. The flaming streets insistently surround us. Personal activism is very much a part of the mechanism that turns this generation on and tunes it

---

[8]*Colloquy, op. cit.*, pp. 35, 31.

in. It is quite unrealistic to suppose that the university in
such a context can avoid becoming activist! Already in dis-
cussing the impact of activism on professional cool, some of
the dangers in too eager and too total an immersion in street
politics have been stressed.

An indiscriminate rush to activism can actually constrict
rather than enlarge the freedom of a university's persons to
make that kind of civic contribution which ideally a university can best make. When one stands too close to and becomes emotionally part of a highly controversial community
issue, objectivity and balance are difficult. It is not at all a
question here, or anywhere else in this book, of shunning
empathy and common sweat with what and who is in our
streets. It is a question of remaining alert to the astigmatism
that can blur and blind in those streets, just as much as it
can at city hall or at mercantile banquets. It is a question
of watching for the point where boundaries are over-ridden
and the heart too blindly impacts on the head. Because of
this new emotional and personalist element in involvement,
the university must safeguard with increased concern the
right of its persons to dissent, if they wish, from the particular stance of any minority of its members on a civic issue
without being subject to punishment for their non-conform-
ity. Were such a situation to happen and the university to
divide into bitterly hostile and domineering partisan camps
on a community issue, scholarship is hardly more possible
than it is in a situation where town and gown simply do not
speak to each other.

Awareness of the pitfalls, however, in no way diminishes
the urgency for a new university commitment in metropolis.
The church-associated university will have its special addi-

tional concerns, but it cannot escape the reasoning which suggests such urgency. And it must read the general record.

> At no time in modern history have the opportunity and need for a major American advance through higher education been as great as they are now. . . . The potential of the university in solving the problems of our society has been dramatically proven. . . . Calls for the college and university to help our society find solutions for its multiple problems and to exercise the leadership for which their staffs are uniquely qualified have multiplied.[9]

There are a number of aspects to this matter. Relying in many cases on recent remarks on university campuses, they can be detailed roughly as follows.

First, the needs of metropolis are so desperate, so intricate, so total, that all institutions and media for learning must be mustered to meet them. Surely there is an extraordinarily critical role for its universities to speak to and in a generation which has been characterized as subject, at home and abroad, to "showers of violence. . . . There are highly combustible substances gathered in our society. It is a time of trouble [and] a time of testing."[10] That role is especially evident in metropolis. HUD's Charles Haar put it well:

> These problems are difficult, complex, and much different from the traditional academic study. They usually involve disparate skills, sciences, and disciplines. They are not neat, dis-

---

[9]Joint Statement of American Association of State Colleges and Universities and Land-Grant Colleges and American Association of State Colleges and Universities, after their November 12-15, 1967, session at Columbus, Ohio.

[10]Senator Mike Mansfield, address at St. John's University, Jamaica, New York, May 15, 1968.

crete subjects for exploration; few urban problems have tidy beginnings, endings, or margins. Almost without exception they will require interdisciplinary approaches. And more and more we will be calling for generalists rather than technical skills, for broad approaches that deal with the city as it is—diverse and difficult, a rich confused tapestry of man's best and most base ideas and motives.[11]

Former Vice-President Humphrey added:

University expertise is urgently needed for the solution of dozens of complex problems—problems of transportation, of housing, of management, of law enforcement, of urban and area planning, of public welfare—yes, and of human relations. The university can and should become an integral, catalytic part of the community.[12]

Already in 1848 in his *Report to the Massachusetts Board of Education*, Horace Mann had called education "beyond all other devices of human origin—the value wheel of the social machinery." There seems no room for doubt but what as society becomes more and more metropolitan, so must the university. Spoken in an almost prophetic dimension, the remarks of Notre Dame's Father Hesburgh in the winter of 1967 add another aspect to the matter:

Here the name of the game is peace, not conflict. Only in the university community can there be the national and civil discourse that builds bridges rather than widens the gulfs of

---

[11]Charles M. Haar, then Assistant Secretary for Metropolitan Development, Department of Housing and Urban Development, "The Urban University: Challenge and Response," address delivered at Lake Erie College, Painesville, Ohio, February 28, 1968.

[12]At Temple University convocation, Philadelphia, Pennsylvania, June 16, 1966.

misunderstanding. If this cannot be done here, then the human situation is hopeless and we must resign ourselves to hatred, noise, violence, rancor.[13]

Second, a new metropolitan involvement on the part of the university is a two-way street. The university needs metropolis as much as metropolis needs the university. While not yet fully developed in terms of community change, the feedback aspect of science and technology in the public sector on the nation's universities has already found its recorders:

> While the academic community is thus playing a leading role in the space effort, the space program in turn is exerting a significant and beneficial influence on education and science. New approaches to established disciplines have appeared and there has been a tremendous increase in interdisciplinary research activity. . . . In the conquest of space, men, ideas and materials are pushed beyond previous limits and capabilities. The seemingly impossible is brought within the range of daily employment.[14]

Quite apart from the key question of public support, the university must be relevant to the real world around it; and that world, in numbers, in attitudes, in problems is increasingly metropolitan. Too much relevance, the wrong kind or intensity of relevance, could be dangerous. But relevance itself is essential. A university which neglects the universe from which its students come to it, to which they must return, and in which it is, cannot survive. Were it to seek such

[13]Rev. Theodore M. Hesburgh, C.S.C., address at Notre Dame, Indiana, 125th anniversary convocation, December 9, 1967.

[14]Dr. George E. Mueller, Associate Administrator for Manned Space Flight, NASA, address at Purdue University, Lafayette, Indiana, May 12, 1968.

an existence, it could create a death-of-learning psychosis not unlike the death-of-God psychosis which was spawned by the presumption that "religion" was no longer real. This requirement of conceptual relevance has, thus, a vital service as well as an obvious survival component. To return to the analogy of "science": "This extraordinary technological and material evolution . . . expresses a way of life and thought that has been generally available only to a minority among us. . . . A world so deeply committed to science cannot survive with a vast majority of its population intellectually and esthetically alienated from science."[15] Former President Johnson's Special Assistant and Adviser on Science, Dr. Donald F. Hornig, put it this way: "What is required now, it seems to me, is to educate all of our people—to make them aware of the promise of science, the perils of its misuse, and the possibilities it offers us for totally new approaches to many of the problems which beset us."[16]

But if science is universally important, so is metropolis. If more and more men need to empathize and wrestle with metropolis, more and more universities need to empathize and wrestle with metropolis. A university which does not prepare and project for metropolis runs the risk of becoming itself a massive exercise in dilettantism from which the interest and enthusiasm (and support) of real men and concerned students more and more depart. There is, of course, a further dimension. Metropolis is a great laboratory for testing the principles as well as the techniques which a university teaches. As the *Report of the World Student Christian*

---

[15]David Hawkins, in *Daedalus* (Summer, 1965), p. 542.
[16]Address at University of Puget Sound, Tacoma, Washington, April 21, 1968.

Fellowship expresses it, "University education [must] become a continuum with society rather than the traditional parenthesis in life."[17] The words of Mr. Haar are clearly suggestive of a university feedback from metropolis as well as a university in-put into metropolis:

Unless our urban universities come to grips with the substantial urban problems of our age, they can only retreat and, like the catatonic individual, turn their faces to the wall. The rewards are sufficient to warrant the risk. For cities are where the action is. They are exciting, vital places that can attract and direct the restless energies of youth into productive channels. By involving themselves in urban affairs universities can vastly enrich their curricula, and seize new opportunities for research, study and development activities of all kinds.[18]

Third, the university's involvement in metropolis must be more than a proclamation of intent, and it must mean much more than simply expanding the compartmented and narrowly technical training of particular urban professionals. As with the churches, a university which convokes an elaborate press conference and says it is now relevant has only just begun to fight. A whole reassessment and restructuring of its ideas and its organization is required before those words have any meaning at all. On the second aspect of this point, it has often been suggested that education is much more than an assembly of particular data in special fields of scholarship. The educated man must be primarily a putter-together, able and accustomed to synthesize knowledge and experiences from many sources into a coherent whole. It is in this

---

[17]*Report of the World Student Christian Fellowship.*
[18]Haar, *op. cit.*

area that the university in metropolis can be critically helpful.

It is quite true, of course, that universities have not always developed to the full their universal potential. Oak Ridge's Alvin M. Weinberg, in fact, points up the university's "narrow disciplinarity."[19] Contrasting national laboratories with universities, he faults the latter for a persistent divisiveness in their approach to science:

> No judgment of the relative value of a universe can be made from the narrow base of that universe. Values are established from without a universe of discourse. . . . Thus, our science tends to become more fragmented and more narrowly puristic because its practitioners, harried as they are by the social pressures of the university community, have little time to view what they do from a universe other than their own.[20]

This may be an accurate assessment, but it need not be and it should not be. The university by definition should be a place of congress and correlation, where particular values are tested, challenged, and constantly re-structured. Perhaps the Very Reverend Paul Reinert, S.J., President of St. Louis University, had something like this in mind when he spoke of the university's new Urban Center:

> The Urban Center will enable St. Louis University to give a dramatic focus to its present urban activities and to expand these activities within a unified program. In keeping with the general purpose of the University as a community of scholars, research in urban problems, urban methodology and solutions

---

[19]Alvin M. Weinberg, *Reflections on Big Science* (Cambridge, Massachusetts: MIT Press, 1967), p. 156.
[20]*Ibid.*, p. 160.

to urban problems become additional vital functions of the Center. We believe that in establishing a Center with these goals, the University will take a new step toward fulfilling its historic commitment to the St. Louis community.[21]

Dr. Klotsche accents the relative spread of university time and urgency of response as against pressures on the working professional: "The university scholar has time on his side and can bring perspectives to the urban scene in a way impossible for the policy maker and urban practitioner who needs quick answers and immediate responses to specific questions."[22]

Dean Stone notes the width of a university's potential contribution to metropolis: "Only in a large comprehensive university is it possible to bring together all the fields of knowledge, research and teaching necessary to deal with increasingly complex urban problems."[23]

A further demonstration of the comprehensive unitive quality possible, though perhaps not always realized, in university education can be discovered in Cardinal Newman's *Idea of a University*. He argues first against the notion that a narrowly conceived "utility" can be the primary end of university training. He remarks, next, on the integration of professional utility into the full scope of a university's purpose. This, he says, can be both proper and beneficial as well for the university as for the professional. He likens the situation to the relationship of general "bodily health" to the par-

[21]St. Louis University, *Alumni Focus* (March, 1968).

[22]Dr. J. Martin Klotsche, Address to the 42nd Annual Congress of Cities, Detroit, Michigan, July 24-28, 1965.

[23]Donald C. Stone, Dean of the Graduate School of Public and International Affairs, University of Pittsburgh, *Civil Service Journal* (October-December, 1967), p. 8.

ticular activity of the several members of the human body. As health is essential to the continuing success of man, so university training can be most helpful to the prospective professional, and this quite beyond any particular skill it may develop in him:

> There will be this distinction as regards a professor of law, or of medicine [etc.] in a university and out of it, that out of a university he is in danger of being absorbed and narrowed by his pursuit and of giving lectures which are the lectures of nothing more than a lawyer, a physician [etc.], whereas in the university he will just know where he and his science stand. He has come to it, as it were, from a height; he has taken a survey of all knowledge; he is kept from extravagance by the very rivalry of other studies; he has gained from them a special illumination and largeness of mind and freedom of self-possession; and he treats his own in consequence with a philosophy.[24]

So far the subject has been university in metropolis. Add the variable of church association, and what happens? What does the fact that a university is church-associated add to or subtract from those metropolitan relationships I have detailed above? Anything? Nothing? Everything? Clearly, at least, all that has been put down here about opportunity, responsibility, and pitfalls applies with equal urgency to the church-affiliated university. There is room for debate as to the differing scope of community responsibility as between a land grant and a private university. There is no room for debate as to the compulsion on all universities in metropolis today to help!

---

[24]John Henry Cardinal Newman, *The Idea of a University*, Discourse VII, "Liberal Knowledge Viewed in Relation to Professional."

The history, state, and future of church-associated education in the United States are the subject matter of furious controversy. It cannot be the purpose of these pages to decide that controversy. Should churches have established universities? Should churches continue to sustain universities? Is complete "academic freedom" possible in a church-affiliated university? Are church-associated universities more or less uniformly mediocre and underfinanced? What is the likely resolution of the debate over public financing of certain aspects of education at church-affiliated universities? These are very valid questions, but they are not the problem here. We speak of universities which have either reached or are seriously en route to excellence. Our presumption must be that some form of administration and financial support has been discovered which enables such church-associated universities to continue. Our presumption must be that, at least for a foreseeable future, church-associated universities will be a relatively distinguishable component of higher education across America. If and as they blur into the pattern of purely secular education, they will nevertheless remain subject to the general metropolitan considerations stated so far. The point under discussion here is simply this: Is there some kind of special relationship as between a church-associated university and the metropolis around it beyond the compulsion which now falls on all universities to metropolitan relevance?

There have been many suggestions as to what the fact that it is church-associated should add to a university's purpose and promise. Mainly, from Cardinal Newman on, these have tended to emphasize a completeness of vision, "the whole man." One of the more recent of these suggestions spells this out in what its author apparently feels to be a contemporary dimension:

> The distinguishing mark of this [church-associated] college would be its humanity, its concern for the individual student and his personal development. Such a college would make great efforts to create a humane college environment for its students. There would be an attempt to maintain the conditions necessary for a community of faculty and students which would be an instrument for personal development, intellectually, socially, and spiritually.[25]

I cannot help but wonder just how this noble prospect differs from that of any college president at any college at commencement, protesting the individuality of his college in the presence of the mass multiversity. But, somehow, the idea that the church-associated university offers the student a complete universe for discussion as man and as citizen persists. And it has merit. Everything that has already been said about the university's potential for combining and correlating knowledge and experience applies with even greater logic when within that university there is a substantial factor of theology and philosophy. Ethics, the moral standards, and the why variable are critical, since the problems of metropolis are very much ethical problems and social goal problems.

The church-associated university is particularly qualified to raise and suggest questions and answers in metropolis on a moral level. That this has not been unanimously successful in terms of those who have graduated yesterday from church-

---

[25]Associate Professor Paul J. Reiss, Department of Sociology and Anthropology, Fordham University in *Holy Cross (College) Quarterly*, (Fall, 1967), p. 24.

associated universities is no reason to suggest that it cannot become more widely successful if and as the church-associated university rethinks itself as a societal intervenor. Daniel Day Williams' lament may well be justified, but recognition of it could lead to new hope:

> The significance of the Christian concern about the relationships of all studies to human integrity comes out in ethical issues. It has been said that the men who are in positions of power where something could be done fundamentally to overcome racial discrimination in employment and in other aspects of our culture are largely the elite, white graduates of our best colleges, but they have by and large done far less than they could about this problem.[26]

Again and again, in justifying the survival of the Church-associated university, the argument returns to universality:

> The university as Catholic must be universal in a double sense. First, it must emphasize the centrality of philosophy and especially theology among its intellectual concerns, not just as window dressing, not just to fill a large gap in the total fabric of knowledge as represented in most modern university curricula. The second sense in which the Catholic university must be universal [is this]. . . . Without a deep concern for philosophy and theology there is always the danger that the intellectual and moral aspects of all human knowledge become detached and separate. Schema Thirteen of Vatican II addressed many problems of the Church in the world today. If the ultimate answers are to be found, these must be found within the Catholic university community which is in living contact with the faith and the world, the problems and all the

---

[26]Daniel Day Williams, Address to the Annual Meeting of the Commission on Higher Education, National Council of Churches of Christ, New York City, June 10, 1964.

possible solutions, the possibilities and the despairs of modern man.[27]

But it is by no means only in a wider curriculum that a church-associated university approaches nearer to universality than its secular neighbor. If indeed a religious factor is important to the totality of knowledge, this factor is also more apt to be present on the church-associated campus through the learning congress of cleric and layman, through church-connected conferences and literature, through both clerical and lay faculty. Certainly, as the questions and quandaries of metropolis increasingly demand reflection on morals and morality, there is ample justification for proclaiming a real role for the church-associated university in satisfying that demand.

There is another area in which perhaps, also, the church-affiliated university should be significant in metropolis. This area is constituency service. In addition to the usual clientele of faculty, alumni, and benefactors, and over and above the responsibility of all universities in metropolis, the church-affiliated university has a special constituency, the Church itself. Churchmen are principally involved in its management. Its very existence is evidence of Church concern and support. Its past is replete with instances of religious commitment. From its campus, most likely, have gone forth dozens of ideas, publications, lecturers, conference reports to congregations in many places. If this were an essay on education, I would want to probe into the changing stance of the church-affiliated university toward its Church. It is

---

[27]Hesburgh, *op. cit.*

amply clear that this change is fundamental and that it will have important consequences for the matter under discussion here. I would want, also, to probe again into the difficulty of any relationship through which the university enters into close and helpful association with any outside institution. The university must no more become the unthinking servant of a Church leader than the hired hand of a mayor or a Federal contractor. Still, despite these constraints, I believe the church-affiliated university can without compromising its integrity become a more effective working partner of the pastoral church in metropolis. Charles Haar and Robert Wood have both testified to a great felt need for university assistance to the Department of Housing and Urban Development. The fact that each emerges from a faculty background is not unimportant in assessing their testimony, but it cannot wholly explain away the intensity of the plea for more relevant academics. I suggest, then, that the entire weight of the pages which have preceded justifies a similar conclusion in terms of the pastoral church. I suggest that as the intervening pastoral church in dioceses and parishes and experimental instances experiences an increasingly felt need for new resources of research, correlation of experiments, and leadership, it, too, must repeat the Haar-Wood plea for more relevant academics. And such a plea will inevitably be directed first to those campuses which are church-affiliated. There is no question but what the requirement of a church in this matter will be for more than civics and sociology. Our subject, however, is metropolis. As has been so often concluded here, if churches are substantially to influence the soul of society and improve their own capacity to help shape society, they must improve their own capacity to think society, structure reform, and constructively do it.

Already at the fiftieth conference of the American Institute of Planners, the religious presence was much more numerous than at past conferences. This may not reflect a totally felt need. It did reflect a felt interest. At the very least there was a felt curiosity sufficient to bring dozens of clergymen for one week, in the middle of the first month of Church programming after the summer lull, to Washington, D.C. The Baltimore Urban Parish Study was published in November, 1967. In the months since then, the staff of that Study has been contacted again and again about the possibility of similar plans for churches and dioceses elsewhere. The same experience, multiplying requests for technical assistance in Church planning, is verified by staff planners at the National Council of Catholic Men. There is no need to belabor the point. Pastoral churchmen are saying in great and increasing numbers to those of us who plan—come, we need help, talk with us. These churchmen are not always top decision makers, but at least they seem to be influencing decision and usually they speak either from a pastoral council or from a priests' senate base. This may well be indicative of what could be a most significant direction in the new democratization of Church management.

Response to what begins to be a chorus of felt needs is, however, as yet uncertain. There are consultant groups here and there concerned with partial points in Church planning, or tangentially with churches, while their main focus is on community. Within Protestantism for several years there have been mature inquiries and planning recommendations at different levels in more technical areas such as church building and location, population-per-parish, and community. Given the demand, it is inevitable that the supply of comprehensive Church planning will itself increase.

This can happen in various ways. Churches can create, together or separately, something like a "national laboratory." Teams of experts can be assembled, assigned the task of reviewing the ecology, resources, purpose, and potential of churches in metropolis, referencing and analyzing specific local experiences, and then coming up with general and particular plans. The National Council of Churches in several of its departments is already a national laboratory in a sense; so is the Center for Applied Research in the Apostolate.

But it is difficult to predict just how much these initial, but still often unsure efforts, will expand to meet the new need. One problem is finance. Quite obviously churches cannot pump the quantities of money into these largely behavioral laboratories which the government pumps one way or another into a place like Oak Ridge. Nor can the tangible benefits of a behavioral laboratory ever be as clearly compelling in terms of utility as those discernible from a hard science concentration. A second dimension of supply is through regional task forces. Each diocese can assemble its own staff of management-planners. This already happens. The Archdiocesan Office for Planning and Development in Baltimore is one instance. Offices of Community Relations, Human Relations, Urban Affairs exist in several dioceses which, in various measure, concern themselves with Church planning. Local staff people of this type are important. Their numbers will most certainly increase, and their sophistication. But by the very circumstance of their location and the immediacy of the problems they will be called on to solve, they can at best be a kind of middle management requiring assistance from above and beyond themselves.

A fourth resource for supplying the demand for better Church planning is through annual conventions of specialized Church-wide groups, conferences, and study weeks. Social weeks have for decades been useful in France and Canada. In this country organizations like the National Catholic Social Action Conference have brought together laity and clergy summer after summer for topical reflection on aspects of Church change. I believe, as does Father Houtart, that the number and need for these will increase. But such particular groupings once a year are limited. They tend to involve only the initiated and the think-alikes. Often they lack an adequate staff and/or communication and influence mechanism to assure a continuous impact on the Church as a whole.

A fifth resource is through Church participation in such community task forces as the Urban Coalition. This, too, will increase.

Still, if the pastoral church is to reach its full potential for metropolitan relevance, something bigger, something more continuous, something with capacity, time, and talent for long thoughts as well as immediate crisis response is necessary. It would seem that church-associated universities are particularly appropriate for the accommodation of this necessity. There are at least these categories of need on the part of the pastoral church toward which the church-associated university could be geared to respond.

1. A need for ongoing research in ideas and deeds. What is the latest data on metropolis, not from one, but from all sources? What do the urban renewal and model cities programs say to the churches as they develop? What is being

done by other churches in other places with similar problems, how and by whom?

2. A need for leadership training of laity and clergy in both the technical and the ethical dimensions of metropolis. This training has to be at several levels, though principally at the top and middle management levels.

3. A need for assistance in the development of a structured relationship for commonwealth as between churchmen and planners, churchmen and developers, churchmen and builders, churchmen and the politicians and the thinkers of metropolis.

4. A need for supporting and testing tentatives toward new relevance here and there by particular Church groupings, by Church-public combinations, through ecumenical civics.

5. A need for teams of coherent experts available to fly in and out of individual dioceses to discuss, plan, and assist as these dioceses wrestle with plant, policy and program problems in metropolis.

This is not meant to be an exhaustive treatment of the subject. I have no illusions that further detailing of the relationships I suggest will be easy or find universal agreement. I am not even sure just how what happens in and about metropolis at a church-associated university will have impact on the pastoral churches. I am sure that a systems approach to religion as intervenor in metropolis must include, as an absolutely critical sub-system, the church-associated university. Again, my presumption is that the university is either excellent or actively en route toward excellence.

The university's reasons for and mood of involvement may very possibly differ from those of parish, pastor, and diocese.

But, as has been noted before, we mistake pluralism if we expect each member of an assortment of intervenors in society to act for the same motives and to use the same thought processes as each other member, even though taken together they may all arrive at the same decision. Correlation as between university and pastoral church may be even more a matter of this kind of terminal action than a matter of identical motivation or process. The point remains. It can be summed up in this manner. First, there are urgencies converging strongly on both Church and university to rethink and re-structure their relationship to metropolis. Second, since educational and religious institutions offer generally the best chance for balanced and thoughtful institutional intervention in metropolis, it is logical to suggest that they will often find themselves in common sense. Third, church-affiliated universities are the most appropriate vehicles for providing a research and leadership resource to those churches which, however patterns change, remain at least their residual constituency.

As is the case with all intervening institutions in metropolis, churches must prove their capacity to intervene meaningfully and their willingness to stay with it before they will be accepted. To do this, they cannot rely alone on prophetic protest or charisma. They must demonstrate a capacity to understand the complexities of metropolis and to move continuously toward the resolution of these complexities, at least on an ethical level. What is clearly required, as it is of all intervening institutions, is a research and leadership facility, or at least a facility which can consistently assemble and analyze data from other sources. Even to begin to decide which of the massive data now available in and about metropolis are valid, which biased, which accurate, which tilted, will require a major and full-time effort. Even to listen to the countless voices, to read the hundreds of books and reports about metropolis, requires an informed expertise. To take what has been heard and learned, to correlate it, to feed in and compare experiences in and outside the institution, to build from all this an actionable program for institutional involvement demands even more expertise. I do not believe that even a totally related church-associated university could suffice for this need in a totally related diocese. I do believe that at least a full-dress demonstration effort ought to be made somewhere. To neglect the possibility of associating the church-affiliated university with the pastoral church in a common intervention in metropolis at this point is, it seems to me, almost sinful. The requirement is so great, the potential so obvious.

Former President Johnson spoke recently to all American universities. Surely the church-associated university must hear him with double insistence since its constituency is not only a metropolis which cries out in desperation for help, but a Church which ever more loudly proclaims its relevance: "We call upon higher education to play a new and more ambitious role in our social progress . . . As never before we look to the colleges and universities . . . to help with every problem in our society."[28]

Perhaps Senator Edward W. Brooke of Massachusetts put the case best when he said at Catholic University:

You and other Catholic Americans have a very special contribution to make. Not only do you bear living witness to the capacity of a noble institution to adapt to change while

---

[28]"Education Message," *Congressional Record*, (April 1, 1968), p. E2479.

retaining its integrity, but you represent a tradition with one of the most sensible and hopeful perspectives on human nature. . . . You come equipped with the understanding that, though often flawed, the human personality is capable of mighty deeds. This is a faith which all Americans need. It is a faith helpful in prosperity and essential in adversity. Without this faith the aspiration of man to be free must perish; with it that aspiration will fuel a surge of human accomplishment that will capture the future and make it our own.[29]

---

[29]Commencement Address, June 9, 1968.

Tentmaking

EPILOGUE

The observer affects the observed. Speech inevitably mirrors the speaker. In these pages, the observed has been metropolis; the observer is a priest and a planner. Three identity crises! Metropolis surely is unsure of itself. The planner confronts furious questions of role and reach. Two of these crises, as I see them, have so far been judged. The subject at this point is the third crisis, tentmaking, the cleric-professional.

Clergymen who work outside the usual parochial ministry, who are professionally competent in some area of "secular" science, and who exercise their ministry principally through the practice of this competence are often referred to as tentmakers. The reference is to St. Paul who, still an apostle, made tents. The presumption is that religion can be delivered with validity outside the normal pastoral situation by a professional who, in addition to ordination, is still engaged with some frequency in the performance of his profession.

Much has been written about tentmakers, most of it tangentially, however, and a good deal by non-tentmaking

184

clergy. My purpose here is not to review the commentary, but to state the situation as my own experience suggests it is. I content myself with only one annotation. Repeatedly papal statements in "social action" call attention to the laity's peculiarly apt responsibility for "the world." I have never, though, read one of these statements which was exclusive. Always there is an escape clause of some sort. Always somewhere in the statement reference is made to the possibility, the record, the desirability of some clerical presence even in the more "worldly" aspect of religion.

A few further words of definition are necessary. When I speak of the tentmaker, I do not speak of the man who works Sundays at his altar and the rest of the week at some job for which he is partially or fully qualified in a professional sense, but does so only in order to provide for himself and those dependent on him. I am well aware that this latter situation more nearly approximates the Pauline circumstance. Paul worked at his stitching most probably in order to survive rather than through it to preach and teach. The term *tentmaker,* however, has found such general acceptance to describe the type of situation in which I find myself that its use seems justified. In any case, employment of the Pauline circumstance is not meant in any way to imply that because St. Paul made tents, therefore automatically my type of tentmaking ministry is justified. Again, the tentmaker I speak of here may be tenting as part of his income pattern, but he is mainly concerned with the tent as an instrument of ministry. In his conscience he justifies this non-pastoral concentration as simply another type of consecrated work in a common vineyard.

Most tentmakers follow one of two patterns. They arrive

at ordination late; or, since ordination, they have been assigned to situations which required university study, regular association with non-theological professional societies, and a rather continuous practice of a profession. Scratch a tentmaker and the chance is excellent you will find underneath the skin a man who originally intended to be something other than a clergyman and had got this intention well underway before his late vocation emerged. He will not have come up, as most clergy have, through an early seminary with emphasis during all his mature years on ecclesiastical things. His close associates as an adult will not have been clerics exclusively. There will be many places, moments, and people in his background which are rather linked with his profession prior to the ministry than to his specifically liturgical and pastoral callings. His reflexes, then, will not be strictly ecclesial. He will be gifted, or faulted as the case may be, with a professionalism which is quite secular.

Repeatedly the tentmaker is asked, "Which and what and how are you?" He must respond not only to the satisfaction of his questioners, but also to the satisfaction of his own conscience. At Oak Ridge, Tennessee, in the summer of 1967, the keynote address in the "Science for Clergymen" workshop was delivered by an atomic scientist in a Roman collar. The very first question asked the Reverend William Pollard was, "Do you consider yourself a clergyman or a scientist?" His answer was, "I am a scientist who works in a church on week-ends." Other answers are certainly as possible. At the end of these pages, my own answer will hopefully be obvious.

There are many facets to the role of tentmaking in a contemporary and relevant church. I propose to consider them below, not in any order of importance, but simply as they have seemed to me since I shifted from law to religion as my own life's concentration.

I. It is sometimes presumed that tentmakers neglect the fundamentals of the true ministry in their preoccupation with technique. Tentmakers cannot, it is suggested, be as "spiritual" as their pastoral brothers. The demands of the profession in which they are engaged must operate to reduce very seriously their time for prayer, meditation, and other "spiritual" activity. There may be some truth in some of these assessments. But the comparison is not nearly as simple as it may seem. If one were to subtract from the life of the average pastor all those hours which he must devote to non-spiritual matters, to committee meetings, to house-keeping details, to reports and sheer micro-logistics, I am not at all convinced that one would discover that we tentmakers had less time for "spiritual" things than clergymen in parishes. For both of us, of course, there remains a problem of retreat and return. For both it's a question in a crowded schedule of finding moments free for the personal encounter with the God we serve. But contemporary theology surely suggests that spirituality, for pastor as for tentmaker, is as much involved in the moment of commitment as it is in the moment of silence.

II. Some tentmakers are living *mea culpas*. They seem to spend a good deal of their time apologizing. They long, with great sighs, for the day when they will be "back in a parish." I myself have never felt this way. God can be served by dedicated tentmakers as well as by dedicated pastors. Obviously, by the very nature of the situation, there must always be a vastly more numerous pastoral than tentmaking ministry. Still, there is no place for invidious comparison when tentmaker and pastor are honestly fulfilling their potential. The tentmaker need nurture no inferiority complex. If he does, he diminishes the psychological strength of his efforts. Crisis of identity is, apparently, unavoidable for all clergymen in our time. Tentmaking can complicate this crisis; but it need not and must not be ballooned into a psychosis of uncertainty about the validity of the vocation itself.

III. Irrespective of his church circumstance, the tentmaker stands as peer in a secular profession. What ethical message if any should he bring to that profession? How should he relate to professionals of his faith? How to professionals not of his faith? His personal knowledge of the vernacular, of the concerns and the state of his profession clearly opens the door for a dialogue with his fellow professionals. At the same time, his skilled presence in the profession can operate to reduce his own objectivity about it. If he has a nearness to it which permits knowledge beyond hearsay, he has also a nearness to it which can lead to astigmatism, to parochialism. At the outset, of course, his double situation makes two statements: first, that he has thought about the moral context of what he is doing as a professional; second, that he has prayed about it and discovered no conflict between his ministry and his professional effort. Questions of ethics based on this kind of statement will rise soon. Many of these questions will be individual. Some will be collective. A frequent dimension will be this: Just how does the profession fit into the large picture of societal needs and directions? Again and again the tentmaker is asked to respond to personal questions from his fellow professionals on ethical conduct within the profession as well as on their familial and individual circumstance. He is often sought out for vocational guidance from young people pondering careers in his field. He should, unquestionably, be a light and an example to fellow professionals of his own faith. He must be closely conversant with the ethical problems which face the profession and of its role in society. It has been suggested that all professionals, at least those who seek specially to relate their spiritual commitment to their work, ought to be doing this kind of thing. Lay or cleric, it is contended, all professionals working from a spiritual conviction must reflect an ethical decision, vocation, and the ecology of their profession.

By the very nature of his double role, however, the tentmaker is particularly challenged. Out of his competence in moral matters as well as in his freedom from the usage of the profession for family support and personal advancement, the tentmaker is particularly challenged to professional soul-searching. A further critical question confronting the tentmaker is this, "How shall I, as a marked man of religion, approach the profession?" I can do so with undiscriminating enthusiasm. I can bestow a blind blessing on it in all its record and prospect. I can accept its chauvinisms, its narrownesses, its prejudices. If I do this, if I come to my fellow professionals with total applause, the mass of the profession at least will receive me with wines, dinners and medals. And after all am I not commanded to be 'all things to all men?' If, on the other hand, I approach the profession with discriminating objectivity, proud to be part of it but challenging it when I believe it is wrong, my reception may be less universally warm, but it will be more right. I am convinced the mandate of the tentmaker, in the name of a relevant religion, is to take the second course. It is not his role to stand unthinking in the pits of a parochial profession.

It is not his role to become a good Joe indistinguishable from the "lumpenproletariat," if you will, from the mere functionaries of profession who want only unquestioning self-justification in their staticness. It is his role, responsibility and within what John Foster Dulles used to call "the discipline of the achievable," to raise key value questions. It is his job to back those elements within the profession which, though perhaps not yet dominant, are moving it to new awareness of its total societal and ethical responsibility. If, indeed, the professional in our complex society is called to be a *pontifex*, a bridge-builder, between individual citizen and an intricate public management, then the tentmaker can and must be a leading occupant of the bridge.

IV. One aspect of the tentmaker's role, important, though by no means primary, is what I call the apostolate of the beginning and the end. Tentmakers are often privileged to speak the first words or the last words at professional conclaves. If this is their only share in such conclaves, it cannot suffice. But it is critical. I recall the story of the Congregational minister who was charged to deliver invocations and benedictions at sessions of the Continental Congress during the early Revolution before Boston. It is said that he entered more and more into the proceedings of the Congress, so much so that he was taken aside one day by General Washington. "I'm sorry," said the General, "but you were engaged to pray, not to debate. You have no title to participate except at the beginning and at the end." As might have been anticipated, the minister's invocations and benedictions thereafter became longer and longer. I am well aware that this question of what can be called parenthetical prayer is moot. Once after a national planning convention I wrote the executive director of the organization, deploring the lack of prayer at the conference. He respectfully but firmly replied, "I have long since observed that such prayer at such conventions does too often credit neither to the God who is invoked, nor to the religious institution which assigns the preacher nor to the preacher himself." And this was perhaps true as far as it went. The chronology of innocuous invocations, vapid benedictions, wooden words mumbled in His Name is tragically long. But it need not be so. Particularly, it need not be so when the prayer-speaker is a tentmaker. Out of his own commitment to it he should be expertly aware of the promise and perplexity of the profession he blesses. Out of his spiritual commitment in society, he should be expertly aware of the societal needs to which the profession should here and now be responding. However badly they may have been done on too many occasions, even a quick reflection on the context of an invocation and a benediction suffices to indicate their potential. The first and the last word belong to the preacher. The gathering is plenary, the house is hushed. What an opportunity!

On 2 October 1967, I was asked to bless the first plenary session of the Fiftieth Anniversary Conference of the American Institute of Planners. Instead of something sweetly general, I wrote and delivered a "Prayer for Planners." Part of it follows:

Give us the blessing, Lord, of dialogue. May we listen wisely to those around us, all of them — the nuclear people, the media people, the money men, the spirit people, the beauty builders and the movers, the big fellows in deciding offices and the little guy in plain places. But give us, too, the blessing of courage . . . and . . . when we have set up one viable vision, give us the courage to fight that wisdom through, no matter the pious dreamers on the one side nor the glib skeptics on the other. Give us the blessing inside us of humbleness. Let us know our incompleteness as well as our strengths. Help us practice always a fraternity of respect for our neighbor professionals, that fraternity of disciplines which we preach at the center of our being. Give us, finally, a blessing of compassion so that we may feel the city, touch it and love it as well as sweat over it. Teach us the spirit as well as the statistics of the revolution of instant urban expectations. Help us to share the hopes and the hurts of man in struggling streets, in Levittown and Columbia and Newark. But at the same time, teach us to know and to share the difficult responsibility of the leaders of our communities who must, in limited parameters with limited resources, build as well as believe, reason as well as roar, do finite, imperfect things rather than speculate forever about perfect but impossible worlds. In particular, Lord, make us a blessing of constructive consensus in metropolis. Help us defeat the polarizations which would separate community into oversimplified evils and oversimplified goods— into a government somehow wicked and a pure poor—into cities where nothing happens until blood runs through streets from which reason has been exiled.

V. For the tentmaker who teaches, there is a double challenge. He is not only doing, or at least keeping his hand now and then in the doing process. He is also instructing and, presumably, inspiring. He has an even greater chance to develop an expertise in the conceptual side of the profession. He must stay abreast of all current and predictive developments in the profession as well as in the society it serves. At the same time, his influence can be a chain reactor. He can help move the profession through his students in those directions he feels to be critical for it. In the process of this multiple opportunity, pressures on him will increase, the time for retreat will diminish, the difficulty of balancing his schedule can become serious. The teaching tentmaker is particularly well situated to ponder in depth the ethical dimensions of his profession. He must read much; he must reflect much. He should be able to reach certain conceptual competences which will enable him to enter closely into professional inquiry into the profession's societal context. At the same time, his academic situation will enable him to develop contacts within religion and to help structure a more meaningful Church dialogue with the profession.

VI. So far, the questions have been singular. What is the role of the individual tentmaker? A final question has to be directed toward the possible use of tentmakers at the national level in some kind of corporate association. At Vatican II, the utility of a body of *periti* was amply demonstrated. Decision-makers in religion, as anywhere else in our society, simply cannot combine with a massive administrative schedule the time needed to ponder developments collectively in all fields which affect their decisions. There is an urgency for competent advice based on information, on a comparison of experiences and thinkings, and on alternative proposals for action. There might well be established at the national level in the Church a central association of tentmakers, a kind of "think tank," as the popular expression has it. This association would permit using the competence of the clerical experts wherever in the local Church it might be needed. At the same time, a common situation would offer exciting prospects for a cross-fertilization of the tentmakers themselves. In suggesting such an association, I have no thought whatsoever that it be exclusively sacerdotal. Competent laity ought, rightly, to be part of it. It is quite possible that the number and utility of tentmakers may change if and as the Church develops married deacons in the social action as well as the liturgical dimension. It will certainly change if and as the Church hires competent laity to operate more and more of its secular business. Still, through the foreseeable future, there is no doubt in my mind that a much more effective use might be made of tentmakers if their professional competences were somehow massed and made available throughout the Church.

Bibliography

There are, generally, three areas in which bibliography is required. While it is difficult to select from an increasing literature, I have opted for recent material and have tried to list those books, articles and authors of greatest potential utility. As in all such cases, however, this bibliography is neither exhaustive nor necessarily optimal.

I. THE THEORY AND PRACTICE OF CITY AND REGIONAL PLANNING

Key References:

Journal of the American Institute of Planners (quarterly). American Institute of Planners, 917 Fifteenth Street, N. W., Washington, D.C. 20005.

Newsletter and Annual Conference Papers in *Planning*, American Society of Planning Officials, 1313 East Sixtieth Street, Chicago, Illinois 60637.

Town and Country Planning (monthly), Town and Country Planning Association, 28 King Street, London, WC2, England.

Abrams, Charles, *Man's Struggle for Shelter in an Urbanizing World*, MIT Press, Cambridge, Mass., 1964.

Adams, Thomas, *Outline of Town and City Planning*, Russell Sage Foundation, New York City, 1936.

Altshuler, Alan A., *The City Planning Process*, Cornell University Press, Ithaca, New York, 1965.

Anderson, Martin, *The Federal Bulldozer*, MIT Press, Cambridge, Mass., 1964.

Babcock, Richard F., *The Zoning Game*, University of Wisconsin, Milwaukee, Wisconsin, 1966.

Bacon, Edmond N., *Design of Cities*, Viking Press, New York City, 1967.

Blumenfeld, Hans, and Spreiregen, Paul D., (eds.) *The Modern Metropolis*, MIT Press, Cambridge, Mass., 1967.

Branch, Melville C., *Planning: Aspects and Applications*, Wiley and Sons, New York City, 1966.

Chapin, F. Stuart, *Urban Land Use Planning*, University of Illinois Press, Urbana, Illinois, 1965.

Creese, Walton L., *The Search for Environment*, Yale University Press, New Haven, Conn., 1966.

Eldredge, H. Wentworth (ed.), *Taming Megalopolis (Vol. 1, Vol. II)*, Praeger, New York City, 1967 (Cloth); Anchor Books, 1967 (paper).

Ewald, William R. (ed.), *Environment for Man, The Next Fifty Years* (papers delivered at the August 1966 Conference of the American Institute of Planners), Indiana University Press, Bloomington, Indiana, 1967.

Firey, Walter, *Law and Economy in Planning*, University of Texas Press, Austin, Texas, 1965.

Friedmann, John and Alonso, William (eds.), *Regional Development and Planning*, MIT Press, Cambridge, Mass., 1964.

Goals for Americans, Report of the President's Commission on National Goals, Prentice-Hall, New York City, 1960.

Greer, Scott, *The Emerging City Myth and Reality*, The Free Press of Glencoe, New York, 1962.

Haar, Charles M., *Land-Use Planning*, Little, Brown, Boston, Mass., 1959.

Howard, Ebenezer, *Garden Cities of Tomorrow*, London, 1898, new edition, 1946. MIT Press, paperback edition, 1964.

Jacobs, Jane, *The Death and Life of Great American Cities*, Random House, New York City, 1961.

Kent, T. J., *The Urban General Plan*, Chandler Publishing Co., San Francisco, California, 1964.

Makielski, Stanislaw J., Jr., *The Politics of Zoning; The New York Experience*, Columbia University Press, New York City, 1966.

Mumford, Lewis, *The City in History*, Harcourt, Brace, New York City, 1961.

New Towns, A New Dimension of Urbanism, International City Managers Assoc., Chicago, Illinois, 1966.

Osborn, Frederic J., and Whitlick, Arnold, *The New Towns: The Answer to Megalopolis*, McGraw-Hill, New York City, 1963.

Owens, Joseph A., "Priest Looks at City Planning" in *Columbia*, August, 1962, p. 10.

Perloff, Harvey S., *Education for Planning*, Johns Hopkins Press, Baltimore, Maryland, 1957.

Proceedings of the First National Conference on City Planning— 1909, American Society of Planning Officials, Chicago, Illinois, 1967.

Reiner, Thomas A., *The Place of the Ideal Community in Urban Planning*, University of Pennsylvania Press, Philadelphia, Pa., 1963.

Report of the Committee on Qualifications of Planners, Ministry of Town and Country Planning, His Majesty's Stationery Office, London, England, 1950.

Reps, John W., *The Making of Urban America*, Princeton University Press, Princeton, New Jersey, 1965.

Rodwin, Lloyd, *The British New Towns Policy*, Harvard University Press, Cambridge, Mass., 1956.

Smith, Herbert H., *The Citizen's Guide to Zoning*, Chandler-Davis, West Trenton, New Jersey, 1965.

Starr, Roger, *The Living End*, Coward-McCann, New York City, 1966.

Stein, Clarence C., *Toward New Towns for America*, MIT Press Edition, Cambridge, Mass., 1966.

Weaver, Robert C., *The Urban Complex*, Doubleday, New York City, 1960.

Wright, Frank Lloyd, *The Living City*, Mentor Books, New York City, 1953 (a reprint).

II. Church Planning

Carr, Jack Ladd, "Baltimore Urban Parish Study" in *Catholic Market*, Stemats Publishing Co., Cedar Rapids, Iowa, July/August, 1968, pp. 24-30.

The Catholic Press, Diocesan Re-Structure Proposals, Diocese of Worcester, Mass., 18 October 1968, pp. A1-A4.

The City Church, National Council of Churches, New York City, 1950-1964. See this publication for a continuous concentration on the urban church. For instance:
  i. O'Harrow, Dennis (et al), "The Churches and Urban Redevelopment" (May-June, 1957)
  ii. Brown, Robert McAfee, "Theological Approach to the Inner-City Parish" (Nov.-Dec., 1957)
  iii. Weber, Thomas J., "Baltimore Lutheran Urban Church Planning" (Sept.-Oct., 1964).

Crosswinds, "Center for Applied Research in the Apostolate," November, 1968, CRUX, Albany, New York.

Crosswinds, "Parish Service, NCCM," December, 1968, *ibid.*

Guidelines for Development of Strategy for Metropolitan Mission, Board of National Missions, United Presbyterian Church, USA, New York City, 1967.

Howes, Rev. Robert G. (Director), *The Baltimore Urban Parish Study*, Archdiocese of Baltimore, Maryland, 1967.

Howes, Rev. Robert G., "Baltimore Urban Parish Study" in *The Catholic World*, July, 1968.

I-SEE (Diocese of Davenport Plan-Survey), National Council of Catholic Men, Washington, D.C., Feb., 1969.

Kloetzli, Rev. Walter, *The City Church—Death or Renewal*, Muhlenberg Press, Philadelphia, Pa., 1961.

Kloetzli, Rev. Walter, *Urban Planning; The Church Discovers Its Community*, Muhlenberg Press, Philadelphia, Pa., 1958.

Marty, Rev. Martin E. (et al), *Death and Birth of the Parish*, Concordia, St. Louis, Mo., 1964.

O'Gara, James (ed.), *The Postconciliar Parish*, Kenedy, New York City, 1967.

Scheuer, Rev. Joseph F., S.J., "Some Parish Profiles" in *American Catholic Sociological Review*, June, 1956, pp. 131-142.

Schuyler, Rev. Joseph B., S.J., *Northern Parish*, Loyola University Press, Chicago, Illinois, 1960.

Weber, Rev. George W., *The Congregation in Mission*, Abingdon Press, Nashville, Tennessee, 1964.

III. Religion in Metropolitan Community

Ahmann, Matthew H., *Race: Challenge to Religion*, Regnery, Chicago, Ill., 1963.

Ahmann, Matthew H., and Roach, Margaret, *The Church and the Urban Racial Crisis*, Divine Word Publications, Techny, Illinois, 1967.

Clark, Dennis, *Cities in Crisis*, Sheed and Ward, New York City, 1960.

Clark, Dennis, *The Ghetto Game*, Sheed and Ward, New York City, 1962.

Cox, Harvey, *The Secular City*, Macmillan, New York City, 1965.

Cronin, Rev. John F., *Christianity and Social Progress*, Helicon Press, Baltimore, Md., 1965.

Curry, James E., *Public Regulation of the Religious Use of Land*, The Michie Company, Charlottesville, Va., 1964.

Cushing, Richard Cardinal, three pastorals: "*The Christian and the Community*" (1960); "*The Church and Public Opinion*" (1963); "*The Servant Church*" (1966); Daughters of St. Paul, Jamaica Plain, Massachusetts.

Daedalus, Winter, 1967, American Academy of Arts and Sciences, (publ.) Richmond, Va.

Fichter, Rev. Joseph F., S.J., *Social Relations in the Urban Parish*, University of Chicago Press, Chicago, Ill., 1954.

Giese, Vincent J., *Revolution in the City*, University of Notre Dame Press, Indiana, 1961.

Gilhooley, J., "The Evolution of a City Parish" in *Pastoral Life*, Sept., 1964, pp. 5-11.

Greeley, Rev. Andrew M., *The Church and the Suburbs*, Sheed and Ward, New York City, 1959.

Harmon, Rev. John J., "The Church in the City," in *Cross Currents*, Sept., 1963, pp. 149-162.

Hirsch, Rabbi Richard G., *Judaism and Cities in Crisis*, Union of American Hebrew Congregations, New York City, 1961.

Howes, Rev. Robert G., *The Church and the Change*, Daughters of St. Paul, Jamaica Plain, Massachusetts, 1961.

Howes, Rev. Robert G., *Crisis Downtown*, National Conference of Catholic Charities, Washington, D.C., 1959.

Howes, Rev. Robert G., "Religious Leaders Allied For Civic Goals" in *The Catholic World*, May, 1963, pp. 114-119.

Lee, Robert (ed.), *Cities-Churches*, Westminster Press, Philadelphia, Pa., 1962.

Lipman, Eugene, and Vorspan, Albert, *A Tale of Ten Cities*, Riverdale Press, New York City, 1962.

Lenski, Gerhart E., *The Religious Factor*, Doubleday, New York City, 1963.

Michonneau, Rev. Georges, *Revolution in a City Parish*, The Newman Press, Westminster, Md., 1950.

Miller, Haskell M., *Compassion and Community*, Association Press, New York City, 1961.

Moore, Rt. Rev. E. Paul, *The Church Reclaims the City*, Seabury Press, New York City, 1964.

Musselman, Rev. G. Paul, *Church on the Urban Frontier*, Seabury Press, New York City, 1960.

Norton, Perry L., *Church and Metropolis*, Seabury Press, New York City, 1964.

Peachey, Paul, *The Church in the City*, Faith and Life Press, Newton, Kansas, 1963.

Sanderson, Ross W., *The Church Serves the Changing City*, Harper and Row, New York City, 1958.

Scheuer, Rev. Joseph T., C.S.S.P. (et al), "Parish Sociology," *Thought*, Summer, 1965, pp. 243-259.

Webber, Rev. George W., *God's Colony in Man's World*, Abingdon Press, New York City, 1960.

Luzbetak, Rev. Louis J., S.V.D. (ed.), *The Church in the Changing City*, Divine Word Publications, Techny, Illinois, 1966.

Winter, Rev. Gibson, *The New Creation as Metropolis*, Macmillan, New York City, 1963.

Younger, Rev. George D., *The Church and Urban Renewal*, Lippincott, Philadelphia, Pa., 1965.